THE BOOK OF AUSTRALIA

THE BOOK OF AUSTRALIA

DOUGLASS BAGLIN
BARBARA MULLINS

Designed by
BERYL GREEN

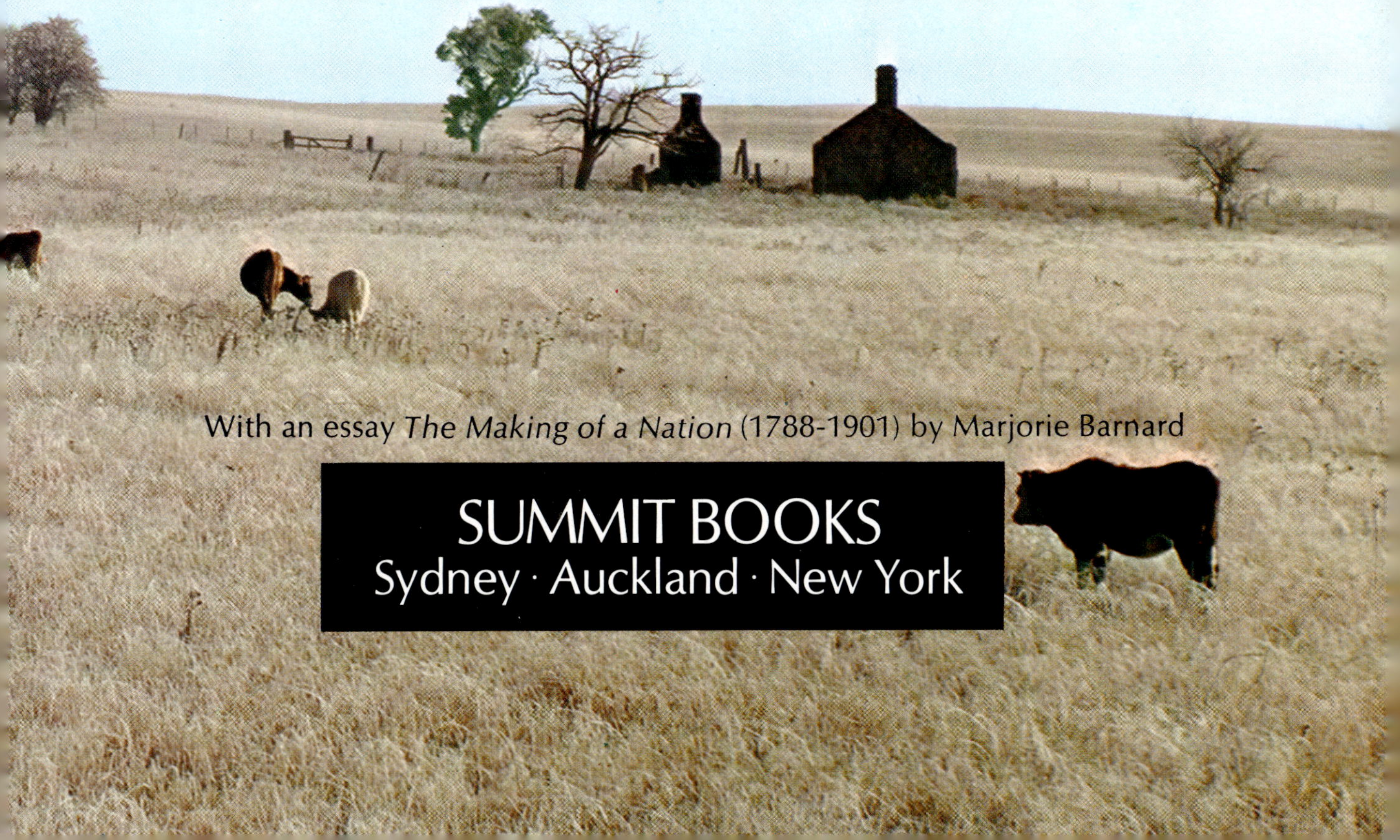

With an essay *The Making of a Nation* (1788-1901) by Marjorie Barnard

SUMMIT BOOKS
Sydney · Auckland · New York

Published by Summit Books
176 South Creek Road, Dee Why West,
NSW, Australia 2099
First published 1973
2nd Impression 1974
3rd Impression 1976
4th Impression 1978 (limp)
5th Impression 1980 (limp)

Produced in Australia by the Publisher
Designed by Beryl Green
Printed in Hong Kong

National Library of Australia
Cataloguing-in-Publication Data

Baglin, Douglass
The book of Australia.

First published, Sydney: Ure Smith, 1973.
ISBN 0 7271 0360 1

1. Australia — Description and travel — 1976 —
I. Mullins, Barbara G., joint author. II. Title.

919.4'0463

contents...

introduction...

Seventy years ago Australian poet Dorothea Mackellar sang of a sunburnt country, a land of sweeping plains. She told of ragged mountains, of droughts and flooding rains. She loved the far horizons . . . Since then generations of Australian schoolchildren have recited her verses, in the process reducing them almost to jingle, so that as adults we recall the lines half-shamefaced, half-defiant: "it's corny, but it's true". Like Shakespeare, Burns and the Bible, its blatant truths have turned to cliches.

Dorothea Mackellar herself was said to regard the poem as one of her lesser works and to have been surprised at the everlasting quality of its appeal. But the more we roamed our country, the more we laboured and sifted our selection, the more we searched for the essential essence of the land and its people — the more we faced the fact that Dorothea Mackellar had said it all before, and said it so succinctly and sincerely that any words of introduction we could write would be an echo.

So, with no apologies but with profound thanks to The Estate of the Late Dorothea Mackellar for permission to reproduce the lines, we introduce this book with her verses, and dedicate it to her memory:

I love a sunburnt country,
A land of sweeping plains,
Of ragged mountain ranges,
Of droughts and flooding rains.
I love her far horizons,
I love her jewel-sea,
Her beauty and her terror —
The wide brown land for me!

Core of my heart, my country!
Her pitiless blue sky,
When, sick at heart around us
We see the cattle die —
But then the grey clouds gather
And we can bless again
The drumming of an army,
The steady soaking rain.

Core of my heart, my country!
Land of the rainbow gold,
For flood and fire and famine
She pays us back threefold.
Over the thirsty paddocks,
Watch, after many days
The filmy veil of greenness
That thickens as we gaze . . .

An opal-hearted country,
A wilful, lavish land —
All you who have not loved her
You will not understand —

Douglass Baglin, Barbara Mullins

the making of a nation (1788-1901)

DROP SCENE

Australia, the *Terra Incognita* of the Old World, the last continent to be discovered, is a study in variety and sameness. It has a hot and barren core, ridge after ridge of red sand, a desert of stones without water, without verdure, then sand again. This is surrounded by lands of every degree of goodness and badness, yielding almost every product and encircled by a littoral of amazing diversity, ranging from the rich lands of the north-east to the barren shores of the Bight open to the winds of the Pole, to the pearling grounds of the nor'-west and the jungle-clad shores of the Northern Territory. It is easy to lose its unity in its infinite diversity, but it is there. Australia is a whole. It has a thousand divergences within itself, but it is not like anywhere else in the world. It is a continent compacted and made strange by separation from the rest of the world for untold time, an island that had evolved by itself and grown old before the coming of the white man. It was the continent which man had not subdued. There were inhabitants—scattered tribes of black men who scarcely progressed beyond mere existence. The continent that had rejected man grew old alone. Nothing was known of it but the coastline, and that imperfectly. For centuries navigators had given the sandy west coast a bad name. Of the east less was known. Tasman had dredged from the darkness the wild and rocky east coast of the island which now bears his name. It was not until 1770 that Captain Cook officially discovered Australia and sailed up the east coast charting it. Coming in from the sea, Botany Bay had seemed good to him. Sir Joseph Banks, who sailed with him, found it interesting country but the "barrenest" he had ever seen. Time and distance were to soften that verdict. In 1788, in the broad daylight of the eighteenth century, a thousand men came to settle this unknown continent. Their destination was Botany Bay, for that was the only point on the whole east coast of which they had any favourable report. Within a few miles of the bay they had the good luck to find "the finest harbour in the world, in which a thousand sail of the line may ride in the most perfect security." There in a little cove, thickly wooded, with deep water for the ships, a run of fresh water, they landed and began slowly, with infinite hardships, to make their way in the new world.

It was a new world, unlike anything else white men had known. Had they landed to the south they would have found kinder country, had they landed to the north they would have found richer country, but their problems would have been essentially the same.

They found an old coast, brown headland after brown headland worn down to their ultimate resistance by sea and wind, with scallops of shining sand between them, where the long Pacific rollers broke in perpetual surf. Just beyond the sea-bitten rim of the coast the bush began and stretched inland as far as their eyes or imagination could go.

It was as monotonous as the sea, as silent as the sky, and all through the year it was the same, evergreen. The trees were infinite variations of one tree—the eucalypt—their trunks shaggy or smooth, the narrow, restless leaves edge on to the sun, conserving the precious water their roots sucked deep down in the pale, dry soil. Between them grew sparse undergrowth, woody and spiny, showing a richer, darker green in the gullies beside the waterholes. In the spring there was a scattering of yellow and white flowers, and the tips of the saplings burnt red like pentecostal flames; in the summer came the red flowers, and in the winter the grey-green sea of trees was unbroken except for some cliffs of grey rock or the white and twisted arms of some tree tossed in petrified agony. It was a land of little water, of lovely distances bloomed grape-blue, of high blue skies, of strange flowers, of brilliant sunshine, dry light, dry earth, dry air, with the aromatic taste of the bush. The birds and animals were strange — the mopoke for the nightingale, the kangaroo for the deer, the koala for the squirrel — the only familiar thing perhaps a crow, cawing in a hollow world. Above all there was nothing for the hungry voyagers to eat. The new world offered a climate that was like the climate of Greece, but no food and scarcely any water, no dangers, but a vast, intangible resistance. They cut down trees, but there were always more trees; they burned them and they suckered. When a man wandered into the bush it closed over him like water and he was lost in its vast anonymity. The soil grew the imported seeds grudgingly; they flourished for a little while, then the sun withered them or they just died of despair. Hostility to man ran under the soil; it was in the clear air.

For a quarter of a century the mountain barrier hemmed the settlers into the littoral. There was a good land beyond, endless grassy plains for pasturage, a rich wheat belt, Australia Felix, but the mountains, though not high, seemed impenetrable. They were not like the other mountains explorers had known; they could not be conquered in the same way; they turned their steep, craggy sides to the sea. Pushing with infinite labour up the valleys brought explorers to sheer cliffs of rock. It was not until they followed the ridges, instead of the valleys, that men were able to cross.

This was not a dangerous new world. There were no savage animals, few venomous snakes. The black men were a people neither dangerous nor helpful, their minds so differently orientated as to make them as much strangers to the first white men as the fauna were. They were not children to be dazzled with beads and ribbons, not slaves to be made the white man's labourers, not wily enemies to attack him in force, nor were they amenable to his civilisation and his religion. They were will-o'-the-wisps, as elusive as everything else in the strange new world.

What the first settlers did not realise was that the resistance they met in the apparently open face of the country was perfection. They had broken into a world fully evolved, a system so close-knit, so completed, that there was no place in it for them. Centuries had weeded out the weak in the flora and the fauna. In isolation they had worked out their destiny. The animals, the birds, the insects, the trees and the plants were exquisitely adjusted to their environment, a seamless creation, and there was no provision for European man, the struggling and the incomplete, with his whole being fashioned by a different climate, attuned to a different earth. He needed all the force of his civilisation to break his way through that silken resistance of a continent, and, having conquered it, he has had to be conquered by it.

PROCESSION

On the 26th of January, 1788, a brilliant cloudless summer day, a small party of officers and workers landed from the *Supply* at Sydney Cove and set to work clearing the ground, which was thickly wooded, erecting a few tents and putting up a flagstaff. At sunset the British flag was hoisted, and Phillip, Captain-General of the expedition, solemnly took possession of New South Wales from Cape York in the north to Van Diemen's Land in the south, and as far west as the 135th degree of east longitude, in the name of the British Crown. While the officers were drinking the healths of the Royal Family, word was brought that the other ten ships of the fleet were sailing up the harbour. It was the end of an eight months' voyage in which every danger from gales, from ice, from sickness, had been encountered and overcome. The total burthen of the eleven ships was only 3,982 tons; they were ill found and for the most part bad sailors. Only the greatest courage and most skilful seamanship had brought them safely across the world to a landfall still almost unknown.

A thousand people set to work to tame a continent, to begin life again in the new world at scratch. Most of them had little aptitude and less heart for the adventure. The majority were prisoners. The detachment of marines who came to guard them were all volunteers, but they quickly repented their bargain. This was no El Dorado, no tropical paradise. A few fish, an occasional kangaroo or crow for the pot was all the sustenance it had to offer. There was nothing for the settlers to eat but the ageing salt junk they had brought with them. Fresh water even was scanty. The coarse grass of the place killed the few sheep, the wild dogs, the dingoes, pulled them down or they were killed by lightning. The little herd of cattle wandered into the bush and founded their own republic. They were discovered years later, increased to a glossy herd, on the rich lands called after them the Cowpastures. The land on the coast was barren, the wheat brought for seed had perished on the voyage and lay dead in the ground, sickness came and medical supplies gave out. Famine stared the little colony in the face; it continued to stare for two years (for it was not until June, 1790, that relief came from England), and after that, for some time, it made a practice of looking in every year about April. Five years later when a Spanish ship came into port and the officers of the colony were entertained aboard, some of them tasted fresh beef for the second time since leaving England. The toast may well have been "The Cow from California". To bring a cargo of grain to the starving colony, the *Sirius* had to circumnavigate the globe. Efforts to find better land were repelled by the quiet hostility of the bush; none of the expeditions penetrated farther than the foothills of the mountains that could be seen from the coast, ghostly blue, on clear days. All they discovered were one river, a repetition of rocky gullies and endless bush. Impoverished by the struggle for existence, a rash of discontents broke out in the community. The detachment suffered from barrack-room fever. The officers spent their time in quarrels, arrests and court-martials. The privates, more sensibly, assaulted one another. Everyone agreed to hate the one man on whom their salvation depended—the Governor, Captain Phillip. He was the true founder of the nation. In a handful of miserable huts he saw the beginning of an "empire". His courage and sanity brought the colony through its worst years. With absolute power he laid the foundations of a democracy, defended the infant colony from privilege as from licence, upheld civil law against martial rule and insisted on the equality of every inhabitant in the vital matter of rations. He guarded every detail. "Two or three hundred iron frying pans", he wrote to the Under-Secretary Nepean, "will be a saving of spades". Phillip built for the future. Within a month of landing he founded a daughter settlement at Norfolk Island, an earthly paradise, inhabited only by birds—and rats. This was to forestall unwanted neighbours, the French, or pirates. He planned a handsome city with streets 200 feet wide to be called Albion—but later he changed the name to Sydney, and the wide streets did not happen either. He threshed out a system of land grants, he established trade on a legal footing, initiated a hospital scheme, created the rudiments of a police force. In less than five years, in the face of every disadvantage, he had founded a colony.

Australia's early history to Federation has a zodiac of its own. The first five years, prosaic and grim, were under the sign of the Cooking Pot, one of those common iron pots that appear so often in the despatches. In the riotous and colourful years that follow it is under the sway of the Rum Bottle, whence it passes for a brief time under a marine emblem, the Whale, to enter one of its major periods in the late twenties, the thirties and forties, under the sign of the Golden Fleece. Next in the fifties comes the Nugget, then a long constitutional period under the Mace. The periods interlace and grow out of one another, for the story is an organic whole, something that has been lived.

THE RUM BOTTLE

No sooner had Phillip left the colony than the rum bottle made itself felt. Government fell into the hands of a military oligarchy, the officers of the New South Wales Corps, which had replaced the original marine detachment, withdrawn, much to its surprise, on account of its quarrelsomeness. Now began an unwholesome but colourful period. Rum was both wealth and power. It came in from India and Brazil and was made at home. The officers of the Corps had a monopoly in it and looked for a profit of 500 per cent on its sale. Since specie was scarce, rum passed instead. The colony lapsed into a happy daze, shot with lightning, and under cover of the fumes the military gentlemen picked up other profitable monopolies and some nice little fortunes. For instance, they all had large grants of land and plenty of free labour to work them, and since the commandant of the Corps was the acting governor for several years, the military farmers got all the government contracts for grain.

It would take the brush of a Hogarth to paint those days. But there was an undercurrent of misery.

In the midst of it all the chaplain of the colony, Richard Johnson, struggled to build a church. He built it with his own hands, assisted by a few men whom he paid in rum, and when it was finished he sent the bill to the Government. It was for £67/12/11½ (later he added another 3d.)*. The Lieutenant-Governor was scandalised. It was too much. He advised the Home Government not to pay it. The Home Government did not.

Hunter, one of Phillip's officers, was appointed Governor in 1795. He was gentle and pious. He paid for the church and tried to force everyone to attend service, with the result that the church was promptly burned down. He tried to control the rum traffic, challenged Captain Macarthur, the leader of the military oligarchy, to a duel, and punished those who had illicit rum stills by pulling down their houses. In five years he retired from the conflict, and another of Phillip's officers, Philip Gidley King, a more masterful man, took his place. He produced some rather mysterious Royal Instructions, forbidding the rum traffic and started a government brewery at Parramatta as a counterblast. But beer had no chance against rum, and government lost money on the enterprise. Captain Macarthur led the opposition with zest. He challenged his commanding officer, Major Paterson, to a duel because he refused to boycott the Governor. The Major was wounded in the shoulder. King arrested Macarthur and sent him to England for trial. "If ever Captain Macarthur returns to this colony I shall fear much for its concerns," wrote King. "Half of it belongs to him already and he will very soon get the other half." But he did return in 1805 and King quitted his Government in 1806. His last act was to grant his successor in high office, Bligh, of Bounty fame, a thousand acres of land. Bligh's first act was a return courtesy. He granted Mrs. King seven hundred acres, which she appropriately christened "Thanks".

Bligh was a quick-tempered martinet, and the contest, Crown v. Rum, immediately took a dramatic turn. He prohibited the use of spirits as currency and re-prohibited its private manufacture. He seized a still which Macarthur was importing and Macarthur brought an action for wrongful seizure, which he won on a technicality. Bligh waited his chance and when he discovered an irregularity connected with a schooner belonging to Macarthur he put a guard on the ship and arrested Macarthur—quite illegally. Haled before a criminal court, Macarthur terrified the judge—who owed him money—off the bench. The court could not sit, Macarthur was lodged in gaol. The military members of the court, who were in sympathy with him, protested. Bligh charged them with treason and usurpation. The soldiers rose under Major Johnston and rescued Macarthur from prison. He drew up a manifesto declaring "every man's property, liberty and life is endangered". One hundred and fifty-one persons signed it—after the event. With colours flying and the band playing "The British Grenadiers", Johnston marched on Government House. It was undefended. Bligh's daughter tried to hold the door, but she was thrust aside. Bligh was taken prisoner. Lance-Corporal Marlborough claimed to have dragged him, like Caligula, from under his bed. The Corps reigned in his stead. This was the Rum Rebellion. But the spirited gentlemen had gone too far. Johnston was court-martialled, Macarthur meddled no more in politics, the corps was disbanded, and the colony made a new beginning under a man in Phillip's grand tradition, Lachlan Macquarie.

THE WHALE

King Rum gave way to King Whale. He ruled in the south. As early as 1791 there had been whale fishing off the Australian coast, till a stormy season had driven the fishers away to the coast of Peru. But others came back. At the beginning of the century the great firm of Enderby was operating in the South Seas. In those days whale oil lit the world. Whales and seals and sea elephants died in their thousands. In 1806 one ship alone unloaded 60,000 seal skins, valued at £1 each, in Sydney. By 1830 there were no more seals.

In 1804, Tasmania, then called Van Diemen's Land, was settled for fear that the French coveted it. It was at first a tiny colony of 73 persons, a last footnote at the end of the world. Its beginnings were wild and hard. The Governor himself spent a lot of time in bed, as he found it easier to bear his hunger there. Wheat was £4 to £6 a bushel, and a cow was worth £25. Importing them even at this

**Throughout this essay the currency of the period is referred to.*

price was an heroic business. The captain of the ship bringing them had to put into Sea Elephant Bay, on King Island, and there hanging from the rafters he found a bottle containing instructions how to proceed with his cargo and where to land it. Whales saved the struggling port. Hobart Town became a port for whalers, a rendezvous for adventurers and a school of hardy seamen. Some of the adventurers went inland and under the thin guise of gamekillers became the first bushrangers; others stuck to the sea. Shipbuilding became an industry, and nuggety little ships built in Hobart ranged far afield. To the north, on Kangaroo Island, the whalers had an unofficial colony of their own, under their chief, Abyssinia, living by barter, their only use for money the sovereigns that dangled from their ears. With black wives and variegated children they tilled the soil between sailings.

The age of the sea adventurer was not quite dead. In 1799 Spanish prizes were being brought into Sydney, and in 1804 the whaler *Policy* captured the Dutch ship *Swift* near Amboyna with 20,000 dollars aboard and brought her into Sydney. There is talk, too, of smuggling into South America, of cargoes of sandalwood, of the French bogey. In 1814 an American privateer, the *Essex,* planned to capture Sydney. Nothing came of it, but in July of that year a whaler, the *Seringapatam,* came into port. She was manned by 14 British sailors who had escaped from the Marquesas Island, the headquarters of the *Essex,* seized the ship and made their way safely to Sydney.

So, little more than 150 years ago, the coast of the new world was brushed by the old piratical life of the sea, little changed since the days of Drake. It was an interlude only. The whaler and the privateer were both doomed. Australia was taking a firmer hold of life than either offered.

THE GOLDEN FLEECE

Macquarie had come to Sydney. He was a man of initiative and energy, and he had more power than any previous Governor had had, because he was supported by the regiment which he had himself commanded, the 73rd Highlanders. He opened up the country, erected over two hundred public buildings, built roads, and, with the help of his wife, a lady of character, corrected the "fortuitous" state of morals which he found. He reduced the 75 public houses in Sydney to 20. He reformed the coinage; he imported £10,000 worth of Mexican dollars, punched the middle out of each—the holey dollar was valued at 5/-, the cut-out piece or dump at 1/3. This, supplemented by notes of hand for sums even as low as threepence, made a sufficient coinage. No one need carry a rum bottle in lieu of a purse. During his governorship, 1809 to 1821, the population increased from 11,950 to 38,778. Above all, he established civil instead of military rule. But he could not have done all this had there not been a strong impetus towards life in the colony itself. This impetus came from the sheep.

The first sheep in the colony had been a mongrel lot and they had fared badly. The idea had been mutton, not wool.

Macarthur, the antagonist of Governors, was the pioneer of the wool industry. He began with 20 Bengal ewes and lambs, hairy creatures, more like goats than sheep. To these he added some Irish stock and the cross produced a mixture of hair and wool. Macarthur saw possibilities. In 1796 the merino flock of Colonel Gordon, the commandant at Cape Town, was sold, and 20 came to Sydney. Macarthur bought five ewes and three rams. He kept them separate and bred for wool. In 1799 he took a fleece to England and it was pronounced equal to the best Spanish. He quarrelled with Banks, who then, to spite him, roundly declared that Australia would never be suited to sheep. There was, however, a wool famine, and some people believed in Macarthur's predictions. Lord Camden, in the midst of Macarthur's quarrels with King, instructed the Governor to give him a land grant of 5,000 acres. This estate, called "Camden Park", became the cradle of the great Australian sheep industry. Bligh tried unsuccessfully to take it away again. "Are you to have such flocks of sheep as no man ever heard of before?" bellowed Bligh in unintentional prophecy. Between 1800 and 1810 the sheep in the colony multiplied from 6,124 to 33,800, and in 1821 there were 250,000. They attracted new settlers—men with money like the Blaxlands and the Townsends—and they soon over-ran the limits of explored land. The sheep demanded expansion. The mountain barrier that had held up Phillip was still cramping the colony. Now the sheep clamoured for a way through. Paterson had tried to penetrate it with Highland soldiers, Bass with grappling irons, Cayley, the botanist, with a picked team of athletes. Now three young men — Blaxland, Lawson and Wentworth — tried a new method. Instead of following the valleys they followed the ridges, and in 1813 they crossed the barrier to the rich plains beyond. Macquarie followed up the exploration by sending Evans, the Government surveyor, to consolidate the discoveries and plan a road. The road was built, and Macquarie and his lady rolled over it with many jolts in their carriage.

So far, under Naval Governors, most of the exploration had been by sea. Flinders and Bass had explored the coasts north and south. Bass, in an open whaleboat with a crew of six, had rounded Wilson's Promontory — "the corner-stone of the great Island of New Holland", he called it — and was the first to sail into Bass Strait. Later, with Flinders, in the *Norfolk,* he sailed through the strait and circumnavigated Tasmania. In 1802, Flinders circumnavigated Australia. Their story is like a page out of Hakluyt, a page with a tragic ending.

Now the need was for expansion inland. In the next few years, Evans, Oxley and Cunningham explored the inland plain and discovered a dozen rivers, not flowing to the sea, but north and west, so that they imagined a great inland sea in the heart of Australia. Oxley, pushing north along the coast in 1823, discovered the Tweed River and farther north he found a white man living amongst the blacks who said he was Pamphlett, a cedar-getter. He had been going south by boat from Sydney, the boat had been carried out to sea, they had lost their bearings, and when they made land again they had thought they were south of Sydney and had tramped north. Pamphlett and one other had survived and they had discovered a great river. He led Oxley to it, and Oxley named it the Brisbane and the bay into which it flowed Moreton Bay. This was the site of the future capital of Queensland. In 1827, Cunningham discovered the Darling Downs and found a way through the ranges from the new settlement at Moreton Bay to the Downs.

In the south-west, Hume, an Australian-born station owner, and Hovell, who had been a sea captain, found new pastures on the southern tablelands and discovered the Murrumbidgee, which they crossed in a cart converted into a punt, then, through the tangle of the Australian Alps, they pushed on to the sea.

From 1825 to 1828 a terrible drought raged. The sheep needed water, permanent water, and Sturt, "the greatest and gentlest of the Australian explorers", set out to solve the riddle of the rivers. He found that they did not flow into the sea, but were the tributaries of a great river, which he called the Darling. Next year he attacked the problem from another angle. With six men and two boats he set out on the Murrumbidgee, followed it until it flowed into a wide, deep river, the Murray, called "the father of Australian waters", and followed it to its mouth in Encounter Bay. It was an epic of endurance, but it was only half of what was demanded of the explorers. Sturt had some idea of crossing Bass Strait to Tasmania, but the sea was wild and his boats frail. There was nothing for it but to return the way they had come, a thousand miles against the current with dwindling provisions. He accomplished it after incredible hardships and with no margin to spare. He had opened some magnificent new country. Sir Thomas Mitchell, following in the same direction in the early 'thirties, proclaimed Australia Felix, and the squatters and their sheep hastened to take advantage of it.

Sheep founded Melbourne. In 1820, Macarthur sold 200 sheep into Tasmania, and these were the foundation of the island flocks. In the 'thirties they, too, were demanding new pastures. An enterprising family, the Hentys, a father and seven sons, conceived the idea of pasturing their flocks on the mainland, on what is now the Victorian coast. They asked Sydney for a land grant, which was refused, so they managed without, and Mitchell, on one his explorations, discovered a small but thriving settlement at Portland. In 1835, another man, Batman, turned his eyes to the southern coast. Refused a grant, he "bought" 1,000 square miles from the aboriginals for 20 pairs of blankets, 30 knives, 12 tomahawks, 10 looking-glasses, 50 handkerchiefs, and the like. The chiefs duly set their marks to an imposing legal document. The Governor at Sydney declared the treaty void, but saw that it was impossible to suppress such a lusty infant, so in 1837 he visited the little town of Bearbrass and gave it the more elegant name of Melbourne. He held the first official land sale. Town lots brought £40; thirty years later they were to be worth £40,000.

In the same decade two other important settlements sprang up, inspired, not by sheep, but by theories. One was on the Swan River, on the west coast of Australia; the other on St. Vincent's Gulf, in the south. The west coast had been explored by the Dutch, claimed by the French in 1772, and annexed by England in 1826. Thomas Peel conceived the idea of planting a colony for free yeomen settlers on the Swan River. There was unlimited land. Settlers were to receive an acre of land for every 1/6 in capital they brought with them, on condition that they spent another 1/6 an acre on improvements. The Home Government permitted the scheme. Peel went out with £50,000 and 300 settlers. Pianos, valuable old furniture, glass and china, all representing capital, were landed on the sand at Fremantle, and there lay helpless. Land was duly granted — huge tracts of it. The richest were served first. There were no surveys and no roads. As the grants went on they became more and more hypothetical. All salaries were paid in land, still at the rate of an acre for every 1/6. It became a farce, and a tragic farce. The optimistic population of 4,000 dropped in two years to 1,500. Whaling saved the colony, and then the rich forests of karri and sandalwood built it a rational life.

South Australia was another example of scientific colonising. In 1829, Edward Gibbon Wakefield lay, not too uncomfortably, in Newgate Prison for abducting a schoolgirl, who also happened to be an heiress. He spent his time writing a pamphlet called "A Letter from Sydney". It described the mistakes the Government had made there and how much better everything might have been if land had been sold for a "sufficient price", instead of being given away. This pamphlet was advance propaganda for a scheme Wakefield had of founding a colony on St. Vincent's Gulf. It was to be an aristocratic colony of landowners. They would pay well for their land, and the money so raised would be used to bring out labourers to work it. There would be no labour shortage, as the high price of land would prevent their joining the ranks of the landowners. A company was formed to carry out the project, the Government in England was not sympathetic, and allowed the scheme only in a modified form. In 1834, an Act was passed founding the colony of South Australia, largely through the influence of the Duke of Wellington. The company was to be represented by a Board of Commissioners in charge of land sales. Government did not propose to put up any money. The land was to provide that automatically. Colonel Light was Surveyor-General. His father was an empire-builder, his mother a Malay lady of quality, and he was a man of parts. The Governor and he immediately quarrelled about the site of the city. The settlers were called together, and the first Australian plebiscite was taken. The majority voted for Light's choice, so he proceeded to lay out Adelaide with elegance and military precision. The colony knew many vicissitudes, including land booms and bankruptcy. (On one occasion the sentries at the Treasury were found dead drunk, but no one was alarmed, because there was only 1/6 in the coffers.) In 1841, twenty-eight-year-old Captain George Grey was appointed Governor, and in the teeth of great unpopularity established the solvency of the colony, and it became one of the most progressive of the Australian States.

The 'forties were the great pastoral era of Australia. There was a patriarchal, even a Biblical, flavour about life. A squatter paid £10 a year for a grazing licence. He moved his sheep from grass to grass. There were no fences. Shepherds minded the sheep as in England, and folded them at night. Agriculture was still only the handmaid of sheep-farming.

THE NUGGET

But as the 'forties drew to their close life diminished. Population dwindled, less money, fewer immigrants came, and it was said that the great days of Australia were over. Explorers found, not good land, but deserts and death in the wilderness. The settlements in the north had to be abandoned. Life and enterprise were shrinking. Then came gold discoveries, at first in New South Wales, near Bathurst, in 1851, then in Victoria, the newly-severed State. The world had already had its imagination heated by the gold finds in California. Adventurers everywhere responded to the new strike. There was a great influx of population, mostly of young men. Macquarie's road over the Blue Mountains was crowded from end to end with a motley crew; canvas towns grew up beside quiet creeks; towns were deserted, and the prices of provisions soared. Victorian merchants offered a reward for the discovery of gold in their State. It was discovered, and in rich lodes. Australian place names rang through the world — Bendigo, Ballarat, Mount Alexander, Forest Creek. In four years the population increased fourfold, in ten years £80,000,000 worth of gold was taken out of the ground.

The country gained, not only wealth, but an impetus towards liberty. There was trouble, a quarrel between authority and the miners over licence fees, a stockade with a blue flag, the flag of the Republic of Victoria, a Sunday morning skirmish. But this was a very small incident, and it, too, was a gesture towards liberty.

Life was colourful and rich. These were the days of the clipper ships, beautiful and swift. 1854 saw a record that no one expected to see broken. The *James Baines* made the voyage Liverpool to Melbourne in 63 days, and returned by the Horn in 69 days—round the world in 132 days. Two years after steam entered competition, and the first P. & O. ships came to Australia. Those were the days of the bushrangers, so bold that they held up travellers on the St. Kilda Road, three miles out of Melbourne, and carried off thousands of pounds worth of gold out of the ship *Lady Nelson* as she lay in Port Phillip. In 1867 the Outlawry Act did much to stop bushranging, but it lingered on till the late 'seventies, when the famous—or infamous—Kelly gang was stamped out.

THE MACE

The 'sixties were soberer than the roaring 'fifties, but they held as much progress. This was the era of political development, the growth of freedom and independence. In their fight against transportation Australians had given the Imperial Government an example of their determination and will to freedom. 1842 saw the beginning of elective government in New South Wales and Tasmania, but 1850 is the grand landmark. In that year the Australian Colonies Government Act was passed by the Imperial Parliament. It separated Victoria from New South Wales and it empowered each of the five States to frame its own constitution. The next few years saw the founding of four legislatures. Western Australia alone elected to remain a Crown Colony for some time longer. Van Diemen's Land changed her name to Tasmania.

It was a time of new beginnings. Already in the 'sixties Australia was in the forefront of political experiment. New land laws were passed, unlocking the country to small settlers, the principle of one man, one vote, was put into practice, the secret ballot, payment of members of parliament, industrial arbitration and wages board experiments followed. New Zealand outstripped South Australia by one year in the enfranchisement of women, the first country in the world to do so.

The years till the end of the century saw first a clarification of the separate States' needs and aims—a drawing apart, and then a drawing together, a general growing wish for federation. (In 1859, Queensland had been added to the community of States—with 7½d. in her Treasury—and had waxed rich in a series of booms—the cotton boom, the sugar boom, and later the cattle boom. Western Australia had become self-governing.) Not without long bargaining, the seven States united at last, and with the beginning of the new century the Australian Commonwealth came into existence. It was the splendid climax to a period of growth.

MARJORIE BARNARD

The Land

Red hills of Winton, western Queensland. Most of the country is flat, but worn out ranges sprout from the plains, taking on incredible colours at dawn and sunset.

Minnamurra falls, on the south coast of New South Wales. This unique pocket of rainforest is a national park area.

Islands of Whitsunday Passage, Great Barrier Reef. These are the high or "continental" islands, drowned peaks of a former coastal range.

Rocky shore of Storehouse Island, looking towards Cat Island, Bass Strait. These islands are a continuation of the Great Dividing Range which runs along the eastern coast of Australia; they were isolated by rising seas of the last ice age.

Red bauxite coastline near Gove, Arnhem Land, on the shores of the Arafura Sea.

Stock converge on a waterhole, fed by artesian bore, at Brunette Downs cattle station, on the Barkly tablelands, Northern Territory. This is the land where the brolgas dance, and golden fields of mitchell grass stretch from horizon to horizon.

Katherine Gorge, Northern Territory. Gorges are formed when run-off from monsoonal rains search out the joint planes of surface rock.

the wide country...

Australia is an old land, worn down by time. The mountains are low, the volcanoes dead, long ground to eroded domes or stripped to stark spires of granite. Most of the land mass is a vast low tableland, seldom more than a thousand feet above sea level, which stretches from near the coast of Western Australia more than half way across the continent to western New South Wales and Queensland, covering almost all of Western Australia and the Northern Territory, and most of South Australia.

This is the ancient land that is Australia's heart: a flat arid plateau composed mainly of sedimentary rock laid down three thousand million years ago, before the dawn of life. It is the foundation stone of a continent, the bones of a planet, the oldest land on the surface of the earth. Stable while other lands drowned or were thrust from the sea, while subterranean convulsions heaved up the Himalayas, this great fragment of earth's creation, though relatively undisturbed, is not unaltered by time. Sun and rain have wrought chemical changes, producing a riot of reds and blues and purples which contrast with the cool greens of the isolated waterholes. Wind-driven dust and grit have shaped the mighty monoliths of Ayers Rock and the Olgas, and formed the inland deserts, windblown seas of sand where dunes from fifty to two hundred feet high lie in parallel waves from horizon to horizon. Aeons of monsoonal rains have searched out the joint patterns of the surface rock, deepening them to gorges, great gashes which slash the flat land with almost geometric precision, guarding long still stretches of water and hidden vibrant life.

The unceasing circuit of day and night, with twin scalpels of frost and searing heat, have pared the granite intrusions of the world's birth to rounded remnants, mountains reduced to marbles and scattered in careless heaps across the countryside, almost perfect spheres ranging from inches to feet in diameter. (White men call them "Devil's Marbles"; Aborigines the eggs of the Rainbow Serpent, creative ancestral being associated with fertility and the source of all life.)

This is the bulk of the continent — a wide land, a land of far horizons. A land of cattle stations as large as kingdoms, where holdings are measured by the thousand square miles, each a self contained community with its own airfield, village, shopping centre, theatre, school, church, racetrack . . . A land where rivers of sand disappear into lakes of salt, where golden seas of Flinders grass stretch in unbroken line for hundreds of miles across the vast plains and desolate stony deserts explode into colour when the rain falls. This is the bulk of the continent, but it is not its whole.

Along the eastern coast a wrinkle of mountains, thrust up at a later era, stretches in a chain of broken tablelands and peaks from Cape York Peninsula, Australia's probing finger to the north, down the eastern flank of the continent, striding across the islands of Bass Strait to Tasmania. This is the Great Dividing Range, which shelters and waters the green crescent of coastal plains and extends westward in gently sloping highlands until it meets the margin of the lost inland sea which now lies locked in great artesian basins beneath the central lowlands — the former seabed which divides east from west.

Once again, the profile is low, for these highlands are not true mountains but rather an elevated plateau thrust up from the surrounding land perhaps a million years ago. No part lies above the line of perpetual snow and the highest peaks are only just over 7000 feet; a flat plateau, but by no means featureless. The winter ski fields of the Australian Alps are more extensive than those of Switzerland — the relatively gentle terrain, in contrast to the precipitous mountain peaks of alpine areas elsewhere, has resulted in vast stretches of snow and an almost endless variety of ski slopes.

West of Sydney the forces of nature have chiselled a series of spectacular gorges and valleys known as the Blue Mountains. These are mountains of air; already the valleys occupy far more space than the ridges and with each rock fall they are larger, the breath-catching blue vistas more intense.

Northwards, in the tropical zone, the plateau is clothed with jungle and rainforest, scored by profound gorges and mighty waterfalls. Here it runs close to the coast, in places plunging into the sea — these drowned mountains are the high or "continental" islands of the Great Barrier Reef.

The "safe country" of this eastern watershed is home to most Australians. In our lopsided continent more than half the total population lives in the great cities of the coastal fringe, and more than half the remainder on the fertile coastal plains, highlands and western slopes of the Great Divide.

Green pastures and mist-shrouded mountains at Geehi in the Australian Alps, near the border between New South Wales and Victoria.

Wind-moulded sandridges at Everard Park, South Australia, near the Northern Territory border. These dunes act as windbreaks for extensive pockets of vegetation between, and after seasonal rains are carpeted with a wild profusion of colourful flowers.

The Blue Mountains of New South Wales — Narrow Neck, near Katoomba. These are mountains of air; valleys occupy more space than the ridges, and with each rock fall they get larger.

Pinnacles Desert, near Lancelin, Western Australia. These eroded cores of golden limestone, up to twelve or more feet high, have been sculptured by wind and rain into extraordinarily beautiful and sometimes terrifying shapes.

land of contrasts...

Australia is a land of fantastic extremes. In contrast to the verdant eastern rim, the western shore of low lying coastal limestone is arid and forbidding, carved and corroded by wind and rain and wave into treacherous reefs and rugged cliffs on the seaward edge and sandy deserts on shore. Less than a hundred miles north of the capital city of Perth is the Pinnacles Desert, where stark spires of harder limestone have been exposed as the softer surrounding stone eroded and dissolved away. These pinnacles march in ominous ranks across the sand dunes, hundreds upon hundreds, towering above the observer. This is a landscape bleaker than the moon's, here and there marked by the intricate tracery of a rare, intrepid earthly plant, wind-blasted to stone by powdered limestone — grim warning to the intruder.

Australia has salt lakes and sea lakes, and the still, deep glacial lakes of the highlands. The great salt lakes of the central lowlands are remnants of very much greater freshwater lakes of an earlier, greener time; the fossils which lie beneath their salt encrusted surfaces — bones and teeth of diprotodon and giant kangaroo — bear mute testimony to the teeming life they once supported. Now the fickle inland rivers rarely reach them, and such waters that do are sucked up by relentless sun and insatiable sand. Today they are desolate barren salt pans where the air shimmers with perpetual mirages and the sun sears the cracked surface to blazing white or burning gold. Explorer Ernest Giles, when he first sighted salt Lake Amadeus in 1872, wrote of: "the bottomless bed of that infernal lake . . . wild and weird, with a white expanse sweeping nearly the whole of the southern horizon, shining in the sun." Lake Eyre, the largest, covers four thousand square miles and stretches fifty miles from horizon to horizon.

A warning note: new salt lakes in formation in some semi-arid regions are a cause for growing concern. It is suggested that these are the result of altered water tables caused by over-clearing for pastural purposes.

Salt pan, Everard Park, South Australia; rays of the setting sun have turned the cracked surface to burning gold. Vast shallow lakes such as this are common in the interior of Australia. They rarely hold water, and high evaporation soon reduces what little they do to a hard crust of salt.

Little Austria, on the main range of the Australian Alps. The relatively gentle terrain of Australia's snow country has resulted in an area of skiable slopes more extensive than those of Switzerland.

Sunrise over Cairns, on the tropical coast of Queensland. This is an area of rain-forests and jungles.

Lake Macquarie, New South Wales, is a large, relatively shallow coastal lake which runs parallel to the Pacific Ocean near Newcastle, New South Wales. The shoreline is over a hundred miles and the narrow entrance to the sea only yards across.

In contrast are the coastal lakes, drowned estuaries partially blocked by sandbars and shallow lagoons formed when storm-piled sands pound back the waters of rivers and creeks, sometimes causing them to weave a chain of parallel lakes as they wander down the coast seeking an exit. Most have channels to the sea and are intensive breeding grounds for oceanic fish and crustaceans, rich pastures for wading birds, pelicans and azure kingfishers. In terms of life forms supported, they are probably the most fertile regions in the continent.

The lakes of the high country are either water-filled craters of extinct volcanoes or moraine lakes gouged by glaciers of the last Ice Age. Volcanic lakes are usually deep. The Blue Lake, which fills the crater of Mount Gambier in South Australia, plunges hundreds of feet into the heart of the mountain, and the steep sides which surround it tower almost as high again. Beneath the calm surface of its incredibly blue waters, the precipitous volcanic walls are honeycombed with eerie caves and tunnels. Deep underground streams from the mountains of western Victoria infiltrate through these caverns, maintaining the apparently inexhaustible water supply.

Sheep property at Sale, in the Gippsland Lakes district of Victoria. Run-off rain water from the roof of home and shearing shed is collected and stored in huge tanks.

Preparing the ground for sowing in the vast cotton plantations of Wee Waa, western New South Wales.

island continent...

Australia is a continent, yet an island—"complete unto itself". In the north it reaches far into the tropics, in the south it faces the full force of the cold wild waves and winds of Antarctica. Its twelve thousand miles of coastline include beaches ninety miles long and the wondrous coral coast of Queensland, the forbidding reef-strewn western shore and the sombre columns of black dolerite which mark the southernmost edge.

Nearly two-fifths of the land mass lies within the tropics—much of Western Australia, more than half of Queensland and almost all of the Northern Territory. Yet the variations within this region are no less dramatic than the contrast between the jungle clad mountains of north Queensland and the snowdrifts and glacial lakes of the Tasmanian highlands and the Kosciusko region.

The Great Barrier Reef which borders that coastline in the north is the mightiest coral structure in the world, covering an area of over eighty thousand square miles and extending from near New Guinea to south of the tropic of Capricorn—a distance of more than twelve hundred miles. In the north this great coral platform is up to fifty miles wide, laced with an intricate labyrinth of twisting channels; further south it is less defined, reduced to scattered outposts which wander far out to sea. Between the outer reef and the mainland the water is shallow, a great lagoon crowded with a myriad reefs, cays and atolls.

Floodwaters surge through Standley Chasm in the Macdonnell Ranges, Northern Territory. This is an unusual sight.

Holloway beach, on the coral coast near Cairns, Queensland. The calm waters are protected by the Great Barrier Reef.

Giant anthills at Arnhem Bay, Northern Territory, tower twenty or more feet. Constructed by tiny termites from grains of sand cemented together with saliva, they are concrete-hard and consist of a maze of cells and passages.

Ninety Mile Beach on the coast of Gippsland, Victoria, is flanked by a long chain of river-fed lakes.

Widden Valley, New South Wales, is the home of great horses and famous studs. The sheltered grassy flats are surrounded by dramatic mountains. Sandstone cliffs, honey-combed with caves, rise steeply from the valley floor. Bushranger Thunderbolt found a haven here last century, and one of the caves is named for him.

The western district of Victoria was the scene of intense volcanic activity in a bygone era. The bluestone lava plains, third largest in the world, are the support of great agricultural wealth; the volcanic lakes mysterious and a source of local legend. Some are salt, some brackish, some fresh; water levels chop and change. There are stories of underground channels linking them to the sea, and fishermen along the rugged coastline tell of unfailing fresh water welling up far out from land. The more mundane theory of scientists is that salt-laden coastal rains have caused the saltiness of the crater lakes near Colac, the relative salinity being an indication of the length of time the lakes have existed. Be that as it may, the eerie sea caves of the nearby coast, extending sometimes hundreds of yards inland to emerge as terrifying blowholes, lend colour to the legend. In the same weird district is Australia's largest lake of volcanic origin: Lake Corangamite, whose shoreline stretches for hundreds of miles. It is very, very shallow and very, very salty—a great place to learn to swim as it is practically impossible to sink and theoretically possible to wade from shore to shore. This lake lies not in a crater but in a subsidence or explosion hollow of volcanic origin. Nowhere is it over five feet deep; despite this shallowness, the lake is never dry.

The lakes of the Tasmanian highlands and around Mount Kosciusko in the Australian Alps were formed by retreating glaciers of the last ice age. As it moved down the mountain, the glacier hollowed out a semi-circular valley, pushing before it a mass of dislodged pebbles and rock fragments. When the ice melted, this glacial debris remained, a crescent-shaped mound or moraine which holds back the water and forms the deep blue glacial lake. The great lakes of Switzerland are held back by moraines formed in this way. Though most glacial lakes are relatively shallow, some are very deep; Lake St Clair, in the Tasmanian highlands, has a depth of over five hundred feet. In the same spectacular region is Australia's largest lake, the Great Lake, and a host of smaller ones. It is a place of awesome grandeur, of jumbled peaks, snow-capped most of the year, reflected in the water of the numerous lakes; of sheer cliffs of black dolerite and ancient forests of Antarctic beech.

Forests of antarctic beach, Lamington plateau, Queensland, near the border with New South Wales. These ancient trees grow a hundred or more feet high; trunks are covered with moss and lichen and ephytic ferns and orchids hang from branches.

Red-stained cliffs of King's Canyon in the George Gills Ranges, Northern Territory, rise sheer from the valley floor, in some places for over two hundred feet. Cycad palms and dense tropical vegetation surround deep rock pools of the canyon.

Lake Albino, in the Grey Mare Range, Kosciusko National Park, is one of Australia's highest lakes. This is a moraine lake, and the boulders strewn around it still bear the marks of glaciers which covered them in the ice age.

tropics to snow...

Cape York Peninsula, the most northern portion of Australia, is a continuation of the mountainous backbone of the Great Dividing Range. It is a region of dense jungle interspersed with "wet" desert. The rainfall is high, but the cyclonic monsoonal winds which sweep over the area in spring have blown sand from the coral-fringed coast far inland, covering hundreds of acres at a time in vast, stark white dunes. In the monsoon season, these are morasses; wet or dry, they are wastelands—unlike the deserts of the arid inland, they do not spring to life with rain. In contrast, the jungled areas which cover the bulk of the peninsula are crowded with many-storied luxuriant life: feet-deep litter, leaf upon leaf upon leaf till it carpets the ground above a man's height, plant growing on plant, forest piled on forest, up to the far canopies of the highest trees. Much of the area is still unexplored but it is a certain storehouse of great wealth. Alluvial gold by the ton has been taken from the Palmer River, but the value of the tropical rainforests is priceless. This, the most complex life community on the face of the earth, is its oldest, richest, most neglected and most vulnerable. In the rainforests of north Queensland are plants not yet described, though the area is known to contain many with valuable medicinal properties, some the subject of research in the treatment of cancer and heart disease.

Because their riches were worn so wantonly, much of Australia's rainforests in more accessible areas were early cleared for agriculture. But more often than not, El Dorado proved elusive; the soil, sheared of its intricate, interlacing, age-old jigsaw of life, proved all too often poor and sandy, prey to erosion and invasion by alien weeds. The white wastes of wet sands in the north bear witness that deserts are not born of dryness alone, and water cannot always make them bloom.

Davidson River falls, in dense rainforest jungle near Tully, north Queensland. This is one of the most inaccessible jungle areas in the continent, and few people have managed to reach the falls on foot.

Guthrie's Creek, Australian Alps, fed by melting snow. Snowgrasses such as wallaby grass (Danthonia frigida) *protect the soil surface of these high places against rain, frost-heave and water run-off.*

Todd River in flood, Northern Territory. Most times the Todd is a river of sand.

In tropical Arnhem Land there are mangrove swamps, dense stands of pandanus and jungles of wild figs and bamboo. The coastline, dotted with numerous off-shore islands, borders on the Arafura Sea and the Sea of Timor. Much of the shoreline is low-lying; sandy beaches and mangrove flats broken occasionally by headlands of sandstone and laterite, and, in the eastern extremity that Aborigines call Nhulambuy and the white men Gove, by low bauxite cliffs of startling red. The surrounding seas are shallow, for they cover the lost land bridge that once joined Australia to the islands of the north. A submarine shelf stretches almost as far as the island of Timor, and the Arafura Sea, which extends to New Guinea, is mostly less than a hundred fathoms deep. Southwards from the coast the land rises gradually to the ancient, arid plateau which is Australia's heart. Over most of the Northern Territory this tableland is low, less than a thousand feet, but in parts of Arnhem Land, that roughly rhomboidal projection colloquially called the "Top End", it is somewhat higher, dissected by jungle-clad gorges, and towards the centre of the continent it rises in a series of ranges to a height of five thousand feet in the parallel ridges of the MacDonnells.

Santa Gertrudis steers fatten on rich pastures at Tully River Station, north Queensland. Rainforests surround the cleared land.

In the north the seaward-flowing rivers are mostly navigable for a considerable distance. The lagoons are crowded with water birds—magpie geese, ducks, and the white ibis, close relative of the sacred ibis of Egypt. The brolga or native companion nests in the swampy places. These are the dancing birds; they perform with grace and rhythm, strutting, prancing, weaving their long necks and spreading their wings. They are large birds, and stately, almost as high as a man, yet are capable of long and graceful flight, sometimes soaring to considerable heights. Here also is the great estuarine crocodile, dangerous to man and livestock. Once very plentiful, its numbers have now been considerably reduced by hunters seeking its valuable skin. The herds of buffalo which roam the Top End are a living legacy of the first attempts at white settlement in the early 1800s. Imported from India, they proved more adaptable than those who brought them there, and reverted to a wild state when the settlements were finally abandoned.

The almost impenetrable vegetation of the rainforest jungles of north Queensland.

Spencer's Creek, Mount Kosciusko, freezes over at the start of winter.

The Olgas, Northern Territory, are a circle of dome-shaped monoliths which rise a sheer fifteen hundred feet from the surrounding open plains.

Lizard Island, one of the high or continental islands which skirt the coral coast of Queensland. A small island, little more than two•square miles in area, it has a significant place in Australian history. Captain Cook spent a night here, after the troubles of Cape Tribulation and the makeshift repairs at Cooktown; from its high peak he plotted the passage through which the crippled Endeavour *reached the safety of the open sea. It was he who gave the island its name: "The only land Animals we saw here were Lizards" he wrote in his journal, "and these seem'd to be pretty Plenty, which occasioned me naming the Island Lizard Island . . ."*

A hardy acacia is the only permanent vegetation in this wide expanse of heat and red sand, Finke River district, Northern Territory.

Castle Rock, central Australia. After rain wildflowers and desert grasses soften the harsh landscape.

An unusual photograph of the MacDonnells, central Australia, showing the parallel ranges tinged green after seasonal rains. During the long dry season these ranges are red, though there are many permanent waterholes in the broken valleys, each an oasis of the tropical vegetation which once covered the region

red centre...

Flowing inwards towards the heart of Australia are the inland rivers which disappear into the arid interior, into the salt lakes of the centre. These are rivers of sand; they have water only after heavy rain. The largest are the Finke and the Todd, which flow in a south-easterly direction into the Simpson Desert. This is the desert that claimed the lives of explorer Leichhardt and his party. They vanished without trace into its wilderness in 1848. The Simpson Desert is uninhabited, and rarely penetrated even in these days of four-wheel drive. It is one of the great sand-ridge regions of the world, where unbroken parallel ridges, a hundred or more feet high, follow the direction of prevailing winds for distances of up to two hundred miles. In this case the ridges run from north to south, and there is only one recorded crossing against this bias, from west to east; yet evidence of chipped flints and other artifacts indicates that in the past Aborigines penetrated its centre.

Sand-ridge deserts cover more than half a million square miles in Australia; nowhere else in the world do they occur on such a scale. But in comparison with other deserts of the world they are reasonably well covered with vegetation, though much is ephemeral, appearing only after the rare rains. The average annual rainfall, mostly above ten inches and rarely below five, is enough to take them out of the true desert class, were it not so erratic: for year after year, it may not exceed an inch, and then be followed by successive seasons of heavy downpours. Deserts in the true sense may be rare in Australia, but nearly three-quarters of the continent is arid or semi-arid. South-east of the Simpson is Sturt's Stony Desert, a vast plain of wind-smoothed gibbers which cover the land like interlocking chain mail, gleaming metallic in the sun, each rounded pebble highly polished and coated with a shining "desert varnish" of oxidized iron. It seems impossible that any vegetation could penetrate these stony deserts, but after rain they are carpeted within hours.

Spinifex grass grows amid the gibbers of a stony desert in central Australia. This is a cruel grass to walk through as the needle-sharp leaves penetrate the skin, causing intense irritation. Stones are coated with characteristic "desert varnish" of oxidized iron.

green margin...

Almost in the geographic centre of Australia is Ayers Rock, an enormous oval boulder, the largest monolith in the world. It rises over a thousand feet above the surrounding plains and has a perimeter of more than five miles. Wind-driven sands swirling around the base have shaped the precipitous slopes. The domed summit is furrowed by gullies and rockholes which overflow during rainstorms and send great foaming cataracts crashing hundreds of feet down the sheer sides. Twenty-odd miles away are the Olgas, a circle of giant rounded monoliths, separated from each other by deep ravines through which fierce winds constantly blow, smoothing and rounding the steep sides. These rounded rocks are sacred to the Aborigines, associated with myths of the Earth Mother. In the deep clefts, where sunshine penetrates only for a brief hour or so each day, trapped moisture of soaks and springs supports dense, semi-tropical vegetation and numerous small animals. No less spectacular than the mighty monoliths of the sand plains are the chasms, gaps and gorges which bisect the time-worn ranges of the Centre: Standley Chasm in the MacDonnells, with sheer perpendicular walls towering five hundred feet or more above a white-pebbled floor only feet across; Palm Valley, on a tributary of the Finke, supporting remnants of the tropical vegetation which covered the area in bygone ages—ancient cycads and groves of palms fifty feet and more high, which occur nowhere else on the face of the earth; Kings Canyon, the largest of all, a mighty cleft of razor-edged cliffs rising abruptly from the canyon floor, guarding deep rock pools and dense vegetation.

The green crescent of eastern highlands and coastal plains which edge the continent from Cape York Peninsula to Tasmania is Australia's richest agricultural land, basalt soils from decayed volcanoes supporting rural industries ranging from beef cattle to cane.

The patchwork pattern of sugar cane fields, Bundaberg, Queensland; burnt off and harvested areas contrast with green cane yet to be cut. There are dangers associated with clearing ground so completely and devoting it to one crop; lack of tree cover reduces birds which could control insect pests, and the soil is prey to erosion.

Rich grazing land at Mount Roland, in the Tasmanian highlands.

harsh beauty...

Australia is a land of harsh beauty, of stark white trunks outlined against red rusted rock, of sudden pools in sandy deserts, of gaunt plants scrabbling up stony hillsides, hugging rocks and holding slopes, leaning resolutely against the elements, struggling, adapting and learning to cope over millions of years of isolation.

The rugged limestone ranges of the western Kimberleys were once great reefs of living coral comparable to those of the east coast's Great Barrier. Constructed over three hundred million years ago by primitive coral-like creatures now long extinct, these are the best preserved fossil reefs in the world. They wind across the landscape for hundreds of miles, rising from the surrounding plains as did the living reefs from the ancient seabed. Cutting across them are spectacular gorges where sheer walls of limestone, smooth-polished by floodwaters, display the fossiled creatures which once made up the living complex, preserved and recorded at their labours. The limestone caves of the area are Aboriginal art galleries; this is the home of the Wandjinas, white-bodied figures with halo-like headdresses, ancestral spirits who lived in the nearby waterholes and created the abundant life there. The deep pools of the Geikie Gorge, now a National Park, are remarkable also for the sea animals which live there — sharks and sawfish and stingrays — apparently completely adapted to this freshwater environment two hundred odd miles from the sea.

The steep rocky hillsides around Sydney, New South Wales, give precarious foothold to the typical hardy vegetation of the Hawkesbury sandstone region.

Ormiston Gorge, on the Finke River, Northern Territory; red quartzite cliffs loom above still pools rimmed by pebbles of slatey purple.

Defeated ghost gum finds harsh beauty in death, outlined against the red of Ayers Rock and the pitiless blue of desert sky.

heartbreak...

Australia, *terra incognita*—the unknown land —was aptly named by those who sought her secrets from half a world away. She proved a land of puzzles, an illogical land, a land where ". . . false mirages go / like shifting symbols of hope deferred / a land where you never know . . ." There was perfidy in her promise, fear behind her grandeur, terror in her trackless wastes. They came prepared to face known dangers in a country of new, and followed old logic in an illogical land. There were no fierce animals or warlike warriors; only the creatures and men who had learned to live with this land that looked after its own, a land that repelled the brash newcomers with stony indifference and sudden savagery. Iron-hard trees defied the axe and adze; stony ground repelled the pick and plough; ancient soil rejected the alien seeds.

They followed the valleys futilely seeking a way through the barrier of mountains, until they learnt that in this land of paradox their path lay over the ridges. They trudged through interminable miles of mud towards an imagined inland sea, hopefully carrying their boats with them over the marshy swamps, only to return another year to face a dry, sun-caked plain. They followed vast rivers to chimera lakes and discovered a land which demanded their whole life, a land where just surviving was succeeding.

Australia is a land of heartbreak, of drought and fire and flood, where years may pass with scarcely enough rain to lay the dust, and then be followed by floods that roll off the iron-hard ground, rushing in mindless fury to desert or sea. Eight dry years at the turn of the century culminated in the greatest drought on record, killing half the cattle and more than half the sheep that grazed the continent, coinciding with the depression of the nineties when plummeting prices for wool and wheat and beef sent battlers to bankruptcy and foreclosures were the order of the day.

This is a story retold every year, somewhere on the vast surface of Australia: a farmer battles to save the life of a cow found starving to death on his drought-stricken property. The pathetic calf, watching from the sidelines, has little chance of survival should the mother die.

Bushfires were a feature of the Australian scene long before the coming of man, as witnessed by the remarkable recuperative powers of much of the vegetation, but as the population expands, man-made holocausts increasingly threaten man's hard-won footholds, and wreak untold damage on wildlife.

Waterbags, winches, even an anvil and vice, are standard equipment on this geo-survey truck before it ventures off the beaten track into the Great Sandy Desert, Western Australia. Australia's deserts have claimed many lives in the past, through failure to appreciate the hazards involved.

flood and fire...

Deceptive green years lured them back, to overstock and face again the black years, bleakly watching "bony sheep, starving, search the puddled dust. Cattle die for maggots on the earth's scarred crust . . ." The lesson is long and hard to learn.

The first Australians, the Aborigines, took the simple approach: they did not try to tame the land, but came to terms with it, and lived with it in harmony for thirty thousand years. Their gods were made in the image of the land—every tree, every rock, every river and waterhole had a name and a story. Living in close association with their environment and entirely at its mercy, they were perforce natural conservationists. There was no bloodlust in their hunting; they did not kill haphazardly nor needlessly waste the natural resources. The bush was their garden and while they did not cultivate it in the accepted sense, neither did they strip a plant entirely of its fruit, nor dig out all the yams. Myths and totems protected plants and animals at various times and in varying degree. Nature must yield so that man may survive, but man must also discipline himself so that nature may survive: this was the essence of their philosophy. They followed the rains and the rivers, wandered the land at its whim, let live and were allowed to live . . .

This fire-scarred eucalypt will grow again! Eucalypts in most cases rejuvenate after fire by means of accessory buds buried deep in the trunk. After rain the charred and blackened skeletons burst into life with a profusion of young salad-green shoots.

Floods after the seasonal rains in central Queensland quickly coat the normally red earth with a film of green, but play havoc with heavy transport. Here a tractor pulls a giant road train from the boggy ground at Min Min, Queensland.

Bushfire at Cooktown, Queensland, is fanned by the fierce winds of the area.

Carcase of a horse near Tibooburra, New South Wales, in the frightening "corner country" where three States meet.

Droving sheep near Emerald, Queensland. The drumming hooves of this three thousand strong flock have turned the surface soil to dust.

Sturdy river gums withstand the great volume of red-stained water flowing down the normally dry bed of the Todd River, Northern Territory.

and drought...

The later Australians were more demanding and less discerning; more skilled and more gullible. They listened to the land's lure but did not heed its warning, met disaster, regrouped, and returned . . . They battered the land to defeat with their sophisticated tools and watched their pyrrhic victory turn to dust, blowing across wastelands of their own making. The new Mammon-gods they raised proved monsters, so that they fought on two fronts—when the land smiled the gods frowned. At the time of writing the breaking of a long drought which drove many from the land they had clung to for generations was greeted by catastrophic falls in wool prices: stud rams were sold for dog's meat, stations for a song. In half a year, half a green year of rain and promise and growing pastures, many more were swept away by forced sales as surely as by flood, only to see the sheep they sold for fifty cents rise in price to fifteen dollars—in half a year, the last half of that green year of perfidious promise. What can you do with a land like that? How do you control the gods? The answer lies between the nomadic life of the first Australians and the science of the second.

Monsoon clouds gather, heralding the breaking of the drought. Williams Valley, western Queensland.

Winter pastures, Gloucester Valley, New South Wales, burnt brown by frost.

Storm clouds gather over Mount Bartle Frere, Queensland's highest mountain. This is a misty region of perpetual dampness.

the rains come...

When the swing of the seasonal pendulum goes against the farmer in marginal areas, stock losses are devastating. In many of these regions wiser hindsight sees pastoral activities as cruel and wasteful; starving stock denude an already arid area, turning a delicately balanced ecology to desert.

Overstocking and uncontrolled clearing create dust bowls and the rich red soil of an ancient land blows out to sea. Wind-borne dust from Australia has been known to cross the Tasman to New Zealand, coating the coastal cities on its way, staining the fiery sunsets blood-red.

After rain, Australia's deserts bloom. This is the recurring miracle of the arid regions which cover so much of the continent. The bare red sands and stony wastes which seemed utterly devoid of life only a week or so before are covered with an unbelievable profusion of colourful flowers. Acre after acre of everlasting daisies spread for miles, as far as the eye can see. Bright-eyed succulents crowd the shores of inland saltpans. Hardy native grasses shoulder aside the tight-packed stones, literally pushing up beneath the feet of the watcher.

Summer storm at Beechworth, Victoria, carpets the ground with hail stones.

Monsoon clouds gather over Weipa, on the western shore of Cape York Peninsula, Queensland. This is the bauxite coast, centre of a large export industry.

Aboriginal stockmen fight the gales of the monsoon season at Brunette Downs, central Queensland.

wind and hail...

For the rains do come; maybe not this year but next year and the last—very little of the Australian desert country has a rainfall averaging less than five inches a year. Meanwhile the desert plants wait. Various are the ways by which they adapt themselves to their harsh environment. Ephemerals evade rather than resist the long dry spells. These are the flowering annuals, notably the daisies, seeds of which lie dormant during the dry times. After rain they germinate, flower, set seed and die, all within a few short weeks during which the desert is carpeted with crowded vibrant colour. But they are cautious, these desert seeds. They are not lured by the transient moisture of wayward showers to break their trust: burst into life only to perish before flowering, their precious legacy of seed unset. Just as they have learnt to withstand months and years of intense heat and dryness without desiccating, so they have evolved protective measures which inhibit germination until they have been soaked by water sufficient to sustain their brief life to its climax.

After rain the desert wildflowers of Australia carpet the red ground for thousands of square miles.

Button grass and other hardy native herbage springs up underfoot, pushing through the tight-packed stones.

the deserts bloom...

Perennial plants often survive by means of underground food storage in the form of bulbs, tubers and rhizomes. They die right back or reduce themselves to a framework of bare branches in the dry season and produce rapidly flowering shoots after rain. Desert eucalypts adopt the mallee form of growth. In place of one main trunk, numerous slender, whip-like stems spring from a knotted, hard and twisted bole buried beneath the sand. Clawed by heat and choking dryness by day, rasped by frosts and biting winds at night, these stunted shrubby trees draw life from their secret, protected underground storehouses. When the rains come, flowers explode in brightness among the dry grey leaves and twisted branches: the blossoms of the desert mallees include the largest and most colourful of all the eucalypts.

The mallee form of growth is the eucalypts' main weapon in their struggle to adapt and survive in a harsh land. Most, when faced with excessively adverse conditions of soil or rainfall, recurrent bushfires or extremes of heat or cold, have the potential to maintain themselves as mallees, and the reverse also applies—many true mallees when grown under good conditions are capable of developing as a single trunk.

Other misers of the arid regions are the bottle trees and baobabs, which hoard water in huge gouty trunks, and the succulents, which store it in thick fleshy leaves and stems. These latter include the parakeelyas which thrive even in the Simpson Desert, continuing to exist when the seasonal rains are an incredible memory, their succulent leaves a source of life in a waterless infinity. The little native pigface has prostrate stems which root from the nodes, enabling the plant to survive and subdue shifting sands, and it carries its water with it in fleshy leaves. Bright-faced it stares unflinching at the blinding sun, striding across the salt-pans undeterred by salinity. This also is a source of food for nomadic Aborigines and other desert dwellers: the fruit is a succulent, slightly salty, edible berry.

Weird forests of grass-trees at Lancelin, Western Australia. These strange plants are found only in Australia. They live to a great age and have remarkable ability to withstand bushfires and drought.

life adjusts...

Most desert plants — indeed the majority of all plants native to this hottest and driest of continents — are careful conservationists, structured over ages to reduce loss of moisture to the minimum. They protect their vulnerable leaves with thick mats of felted hair, coat them with wax or hard, leathery impervious skin, roll them tightly to reduce and protect the exposed surface, even eliminate them altogether as do so many of the acacias.

The grass-trees or "blackboys", extremely slow-growing plants unique to Australia, are remarkably well-adjusted to withstand drought and bushfires. Over many years the stem thickens to a stout resin-impregnated trunk which in some species grows to ten or twelve feet high. It has been estimated (though some botanists dispute it) that the rate of growth is only a foot a century, which would make large specimens very old trees indeed. They flower profusely after bushfires, the tiny blossoms massed at the end of very tall, spearlike spikes six or more feet high, which shoot up miraculously in a matter of days in remarkable contrast to the slow growth of the parent plant. Grass-like, razor-sharp foliage springs in a dense tuft and falls like a skirt around the dark trunk, charred by countless bushfires and jacketed with the tightly packed bases of old leaves.

Wattles are the most widespread of all Australian plants, occurring in infinite variety throughout the continent, inhabiting regions where even the eucalypt cannot maintain an existence. They form the largest genus in the flora of the land: more than six hundred species have been described. They bristle low on hot sand, only inches high, spiked, hard, leafless, blazing gold beneath the scorching sun of the arid interior. They are the dark trees of rainforests, a hundred or more feet high, soft-leafed and feathery, sweetly scented and crowned with pale gold. Vast tracts of country — mulga, myall, brigalow — carry their names; all but a handful occur nowhere else in the world. A wattle is Australia's national floral emblem, and wattle is featured on the coat of arms and coinage. The majority have eliminated true leaves and replaced them with flattened leaf-like stalks which come in all shapes and sizes from mere prickles to broad sickle-shaped structures up to a foot long.

The smooth-barked angophora, *Angophora costata*, is often called the Sydney red gum or apple gum, though in fact it is not a eucalypt but belongs to the closely related genus *Angophora*. Confined to eastern Australia, and mostly to the sandstone country of the central New South Wales coast, its smooth trunk hugs and moulds to the rocky ground, seeming to flow over the ledges.

Acacia cunneata is a glorious little wattle capable of growing in the most exposed and barren situations. It is confined to the south west corner of Western Australia and forms a low spreading bush, rarely more than a foot or so high.

The great grey kangaroo, or Forester, *Macropus giganteus* was once very common in eastern and southern Australia. Cook wrote: "The kanguru are in the greatest number, for we seldom went into the country without seeing some." Today, though there are still reasonable numbers, they are in greater danger than the big red of the open plains. Extensive clearing of forests has destroyed their habitat and brought them into more direct conflict with the farmer.

unique...

These leaf-like modified stalks are tougher than true leaves, more thrifty with limited moisture. All Australia's wattles are golden, but that phrase covers a colour range from pale cream to deep orange. You could plant a different wattle every day for a year and still have as many left over, and all your days would be golden for there is not a time throughout the year when one or another is not in bloom.

It is the eucalypt however that is the main element of the Australian bush. Eucalypts predominate in more than nine-tenths of Australia's total forest area. They mark the limit of tree growth on the Australian Alps and battle the desert sands. They stand waist-deep in floodwaters, buttressing the banks of inland rivers, and hang by their toes from bare rock above the salt sea. Nowhere else in the world does a single group of plants so command an entire continent, nor a continent so contain a plant, for with the exception of a half-dozen species which extend to the nearby islands of the north, no eucalypts occur naturally outside this country.

Eucalypts range from waist-high stunted mallees to the tallest flowering tree in the world — the mighty mountain ash which has been known to soar up to four hundred feet, with smooth straight trunk uncluttered for half that height. The flowers we see have no petals, for these are fused together into a protective cap which covers the bud and is shed when it opens; they consist of crowded, honey-laden stamens, often colourful and carried in massed clusters. Gumleaves all have oil glands and foliage is highly aromatic, spicing the warm bush breezes with lemon, peppermint and other fragrances as well as characteristic eucalyptus. In the high country in winter the white sally stands knee-deep in snowdrifts, carrying ice-coated, green, unfrozen leaves — they do not freeze because of the high oil content. In the hot country where the listless hanging leaves turn sideways to the sun — letting the heat slip through, hunching one shoulder to the burning rays — this oil content helps reduce evaporation.

Above: *Fuchsia heath,* Epacris longiflora. *The scarlet and white pendulous flowers of this lovely native of eastern Australian sandstone are an inch or more long and are carried along the length of slender branches, almost continuously throughout the year.*

Opposite page: *The waratah,* Telopea speciosissima, *has been described as the most perfectly formed flower in the world. The showy, brilliant red flower-head, four or more inches across, is actually a collection of numerous individual flowers surrounded by colourful petal-like bracts and massed in dense terminal heads at the end of long straight stems. Dozens of these spectacular blooms may be produced on a single bush, which may be ten or twelve feet high. It is confined to the coastal sandstone country of New South Wales and its natural habitat is increasingly threatened by the expanding cities of Sydney, Newcastle and Wollongong.*

Tiny honey-eating possum feeds on the heath-leafed banksia, Banksia ericifolia.

Great grey kangaroo.

The alpine mint bush, Prostanthera cuneata; *its delicate flowers range from white to pale mauve and foliage is aromatic.*

Eucalypts are evergreens, shedding and renewing their leaves indiscriminately throughout the year, maintaining the continuous monotone of dull green so characteristic of the Australian bush. The newcomer, faced with mile upon endless mile of gumtrees, too often dismisses the Australian bush as monotonous, misled by the camouflage that conceals great beauty and infinite variety. He travels two thousand miles or more and still, it seems, sees repeated the same trees as grew in the gully behind the suburban backyard he left. But eucalypts play infinite variations on a theme, even within a single tree. Their greatest diversity lies in the trunk, and these vary not just according to species but with the time of year as well. In this topsy-turvy land where the ever-changing leaves are changeless, bark is shed seasonally, splashing the autumn colours of the old world across a southern spring. In an upside-down way, of course. The falling bark is grey and old and colourless, stripped off and thrown curling to the ground to reveal a new shining coat of many colours—butter yellow and wine red, pink and orange and slatey blue, blotched with powdery spots and painted patterns, dripping beads of blood-red amber (the "gum" from which the common name is derived).

Wattles and eucalypts dominate the flora of Australia. There are over six hundred species of Acacia and more than three hundred eucalypts. One or another occurs in all parts of the continent except the most barren desert regions, and even there they form the last outposts. Pictured at top is the ghost gum of the inland, Eucalyptus papuana, *against the red backdrop of Simpsons Bluff, central Australia. Left: eucalypts and wattles, so typical of the Australian bush, seen on a misty morning in the Hunter Valley, New South Wales.*

Australia was dubbed the "land of living fossils" when news of its strange and wonderful fauna reached Europe—though in some cases there was nothing remotely like them, even as fossils, anywhere else in the world. Bush balladist Banjo Paterson called them "the animals Noah forgot" and indeed there are no myths of a great flood in Aboriginal legends; it would seem Australia itself was ample ark, and the seas that surround her sufficient protection from the savagery of the superior life-forms that developed elsewhere.

For on the whole they were a peaceful lot. There were no large beasts of prey and very few carnivores. The mammals in the main were forms regarded by science as "primitive"—relics of a lower stage of evolution: marsupials who had not developed a placenta to nourish their young within the womb but produced them in a sightless, almost embryonic stage and suckled and protected them in a body pouch; monotremes who brought forth their young while still within the egg, and, with neither pouch nor teats, brooded them in temporary folds of skin and fed them milk oozing from enlarged pores.

When man first arrived he also was "primitive": he had not reached the stage where he killed—his own kind or any other—for reasons other than survival. He had no dreams of conquest but sought and found his niche within the existing network. His hunting dog, the dingo, ousted its marsupial counterpart, the thylacine, by superior hunting skill and speed (this wolf-sized creature, the largest carnivore marsupials evolved, was a solitary hunter content to jog patiently after its prey for days if necessary and found itself mighty hungry when the swifter-footed dingo packs moved in and robbed it of its kill). There is also a suggestion that man and his dog may have contributed to the extinction of Australia's marsupial mammoth, the giant wombat-like diprotodon which, on the evidence of ancient middens, was still around when they arrived, but most likely changing climates and the cardinal sin—inability to adjust—were the main culprits. These exceptions aside, the marsupial sanctuary remained unviolated until the second coming of man two centuries ago.

Pelicans take to the air near Cairns, Queensland. These large, grotesque birds are extraordinarily graceful in the air and have been known to soar to extraordinary heights.

Brushtail possum, Trichosurus vulpecula. *This little marsupial is found throughout the mainland and adjacent islands. It is a completely harmless and a very friendly little animal, frequently sharing its territory with encroaching humans—and their beds, too, if given a chance!*

The frilled lizard of the tropical north is the largest and most spectacular of Australia's dragons. It grows to about three feet and the colourful frill, when fully extended, may measure a foot across and completely hide the body.

Another casualty of the expanding suburbs of Sydney is the lovely, sweet-scented native rose (Boronia serrulata) *which was once abundant in the Hawkesbury sandstone country of the area. It is now extremely rare outside the large national parks—Ku-ring-gai Chase to the north and Royal National Park in the south. The Hawkesbury sandstone of coastal New South Wales contains a greater variety of plants than the whole of the British Isles, many found only in this limited area.*

Australia's koalas were nearing extinction in the first half of this century following indiscriminate slaughter for their fur. Growing public concern led to its absolute protection and practical measures such as sanctuaries to save it.

Acacia undulifolia, *a summer-flowering wattle of the tablelands and western slopes of New South Wales and Queensland.*

beautiful...

Set adrift in their great ark for sixty million or so years of isolation, marsupials and monotremes evolved many parallels to life forms elsewhere. They found similar answers to the same problems, devised similar specialization to meet the same demands for survival. Thus we have marsupial mice and blind, burrowing marsupial moles; a spiny anteater that rolls itself into a defensive ball of ferocious spikes like the European hedgehog; squirrel-like possums and possums with prehensile "monkey" tails — and the duck-billed, water-dwelling platypus. At the same time they also invented some ingenious contraptions of their own — the massive tail and great hind feet of the kangaroo, which enabled it to bound effortlessly over obstacles, up to forty feet in one leap and forty miles in one hour — an invention surely worthy of a place beside the wheel. Less obvious, but equally unique and even more ingenious, is the female kangaroo's counter to environmental and other factors which could threaten the survival of the species. In her role of custodian of future generations, she keeps "one up her sleeve" (if the euphemism can be forgiven) in a process known scientifically as delayed implantation. Gestation period is about three weeks, but the tiny inch-long joey produced must occupy the pouch for some months before it is mature enough to make its own way. Its fleet-footed mother, nomadically foraging for food, can carry only one young at a time. She cannot hedge her bets with large litters but does so by retaining a replacement in her uterus, a fertilized egg which remains in a state of suspended development while the pouch is occupied. Should the youngster be lost, a second joey emerges to replace it; should drought delay its maturity, the second one waits — periods of up to a year have been recorded; should hard times leave the pouch empty and the doe mateless, she can ensure continuity of life when the green times return.

The yellow-footed rock wallaby of South Australia, Petrogale xanthopus, *is an agile, prettily-marked creature with yellow ears, forearms and feet, and characteristic yellow and brown bands around the tail, to which it owes its alternative common name, "ringed-tail". This colouration is protective camouflage, for it matches the tumbled rocks among which they live, but proved its greatest peril with white settlement; brisk trade in the attractive pelts early led to extermination in more accessible haunts. It is now totally protected.*

Eucalypt near Geraldton, Western Australia, bows to the prevailing winds.

The grotesque baob, Adansonia gregorii, found only in north-western Australia, stores water in thickened branches and huge spongy trunk. The only other member of the genus occurs in tropical Africa. This baob near Derby, Western Australia, has a hollowed trunk which has provided shelter for wanderers and is said to have been used on occasions as a temporary prison.

The cassowary, large, flightless Australian bird second in size only to the emu and more brightly coloured, occurs in north-eastern Queensland and New Guinea. Like the emu, the male cassowary broods the eggs and looks after the chicks.

The wide-eyed, nocturnal spotted cuscus of north Queensland has been described as the marsupial equivalent of the monkey; it has a prehensile tail, scaly and partially hairless on the outer end. Largest of Australia's possums.

grotesque...

Though Australia is the acknowledged home of marsupials, they are recorded as fossils elsewhere in the world and living representatives still exist, to a limited degree, in central and south America. The strange egg-laying mammals known as monotremes, however, are a life form unique to Australia and unknown even as fossils anywhere else in the world. When the first specimen of the platypus reached Europe it was understandably regarded as a possible practical joke—half bird, half mammal, furred and web-footed, with a duck's bill and a beaver's tail! But not a bird, for it had neither wings nor feathers; no mammal either, for it laid eggs; nor could it be a reptile, for it was warm-blooded! Surely one of those *monstrous impostures which the artful Chinese then practised on European adventurers—these oriental taxidermists were quite notorious for their skill in constructing non-existent animals for sale to credulous seamen, such as the so-called "eastern mermaid" . . . consisting of the forepart of a monkey skilfully stitched to the tail of a fish* to quote a contemporary anatomist. Zoologist Ellis Troughton comments that it was just as well for the sanity of the naturalists of the day that the even more paradoxical fact that the platypus suckled its young into the bargain was not then known, being obscured by the absence of orthodox teats!

The People

People are a product of two things: the land and their history. Australia has moulded the later migrations of humanity as surely as she did the first. Isolation plays a major part. Smallest continent, largest island — take your pick; no matter which, Australia is the largest area on the face of the earth with one people, one language, and no frontiers other than the seas that surround her. No major wars have been fought on her soil. The land itself has always been the major preoccupation, the challenge and the uniting force.

The black Australians arrived in several waves over a number of thousands of years, and the land absorbed them, moulded them and made them one. White Australians arrived over the last two centuries. They came as criminal deportees guarded by troops whose salaries were measured in rum; as penniless representatives of the English middle and working classes lured from their homeland by bright hopes and the promise of a more expansive future; as gold-seeking adventurers from all corners of the globe. Almost without exception they found the land unspeakably hostile, but most of them remained to live in economic circumstances well beyond the reach of their English contemporaries. And the land measured them, moulded them, and fashioned them to its ways. This motley collection of world-roaming rebels wrote the land's history, so that the land and the human story combined, assumed an identity so overpowering that it claimed most who came, creating a distinctive national character in less than two centuries.

The men who made Australia were in the main rebels. The convicts included many whose only crime was to struggle against injustice — trade-unionists from Tolpuddle, Scottish Martyrs, Irish patriots, Chartists, naval mutineers and hungry, rioting farm labourers — protesters one and all. Others were rebels in the making, transported for insignificant offences by a ruling class casting terrified eyes across the Channel where the rumbles of revolution grew louder every day, so that the smallest transgression of law presaged disaster and the slightest tilt at authority spelt revolt. The adventurous soldiers who accompanied them were rebels also, made more so by the wide seas that separated them from established authority; the settlers that followed were the boldest and most determined, the gold-diggers and sealers who joined them, the footloose, adventurous wanderers of the wide world.

Australians are a practical lot, taking their country's climatic sleight of hand with good humour, be it rain or searing heat. Cattle sale at Oatlands, Tasmania. Sales such as this are also important social "get-togethers" for country people who may live several miles from their nearest neighbours.

Young Australians in the surf at Bondi, New South Wales, a world-renowned beach within a few miles of the centre of Sydney. There are magnificent surfing beaches on almost every part of Australia's twelve thousand mile coastline, and since the majority of the population lives on the coastal fringe, most Australians have easy access to them. This is perhaps why Australia has produced many of the world's foremost swimming champions.

Some, however, sunbake in the streets of the inner suburbs, seeking and finding entertainment in the passing scene. With the instinctive affinity all children have for animals, these seek the company of the street-cleaner's horse, while all solemnly enjoy a refreshment break. The horse as a form of working transport is still very much alive in Balmain, an unusual and proud suburb of Sydney.

LIC. VIC.
XXXX
NOW
Bottle
Meals.

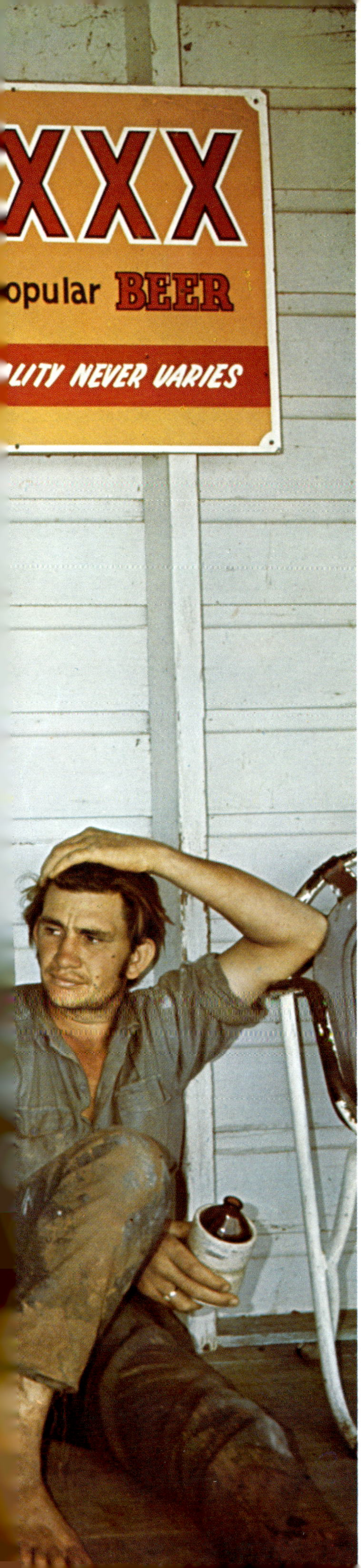

imperturbable...

In their face-to-face encounter with the old, vast land, the sombre enigma where even the birds laughed outrageously at their efforts to tame it, they added another trait to the national character — an imperturbable ability to take what comes. The idiom rings with their "blind eye" optimism — "just around the corner" "over the next hill" "you should have been here yesterday" "it'll be better next season"; the bush ballads sing of their acceptance: "Together we'll roam from our drought-stricken home/ It seems that such things have to be . . ." and "When the country was cursed with the drought at its worst/ And the cattle were dying in scores/ Though down on my luck, I kept up my pluck/ Thinking justice might temper the laws . . ."

The easy-going nature that enables the Australian to take what comes in the way of adversity is also expressed in what Craig McGregor calls a "purposeful hedonism". Beer-drinking is a national pastime, and the daily gathering at the pub after "knock-off" an important social activity in the lives of most workers. Here they enjoy easy camaraderie with their mates, swop gossip, "chew the rag", conduct business, secure jobs, make sales and wager bets on anything from the speed of a horse to the fall of a penny.

Australian pubs produced their own brand of literature, usually bragging of one's capacity for something or other, be it shearing, or drinking or what-have-you. They have also produced their own brand of character: the Jimmy Woodser, for example. Australians do not like drinking alone; this unhappy state is referred to variously as: "on his Pat Malone" (rhyming slang for "on his own", sometimes shortened to "on his Pat"); "drinking with the flies", or doing a Jimmy Woodser.

Australians like their beer. After the day's work it is the tradition to have a middy of old or a schooner of new with their mates. The same groups tend to stick to the same pubs and there is easy camaraderie all round. The Hamilton Hotel, in central Queensland, has rare character and is full of characters.

The origin of Jimmy Woodser is not clear, but two bush poets refer to him. In 1892 Barcroft Boake wrote "Jimmy Wood", the tale of a lonely Briton with one mission in life: to put an end to the Australian habit of "shouting", or buying rounds of drinks. Boasted Jimmy Wood:

"I never pay for others, nor do I
Take drink from them, and never, never wood, sir
One man one liquor! though I have to die
A martyr to my faith, that's Jimmy Wood, sir!"

Around about the same time Henry Lawson (1867-1922) wrote "The Old Jimmy Woodser":

"The old Jimmy Woodser comes into the bar
Unwelcomed, unnoticed, unknown,
Too old and too odd to be drunk with, by far;
So he glides to the end
  where the lunch-baskets are
And they say that he tipples alone."

Bill Wannan, veteran collector of Australian folklore, cites another possible origin of "Jimmy Woodser": that it is related to an old Sydney slang expression, "Johnny Warder", meaning a good-for-nothing trying to cadge drinks. (John Ward was a Sydney publican who kept a low tavern in the early days.) The connection between a dedicated lone drinker and a bar cadger may seem slight, but not so when one accepts that the system of "shouting" is linked with the second cardinal rule of Australian pub-drinking: every man must pay his way, so that the lone drinker is eyed with suspicion as one seeking to evade his "turn". "Treating a cobber to a drink" carries the unspoken compulsion of return "shouts"—an intimidating prospect, physically if not financially, if the group be large; but drinking on your own is unthinkable—the mark of the outcast. Thus do the sons of rebels become conformist.

Picnickers at the Myall Lakes, just north of Newcastle, New South Wales, a unique area of natural bush which Australians are determined to retain as a national park. Portable barbecue replaces the traditional open fire, as a precaution against bushfire.

Skiers on the summit of Kosciusko, looking towards Mount Twynam. The relatively gentle terrain of Australia's snowfields has encouraged the development of ski touring as a practical and popular pastime. This is the Nordic type of skiing (langlauffing) as opposed to down-hill skiing. Marathon langlauf events are held in the Australian Alps.

Paper boys at Wagga, New South Wales, load up on a frosty winter morning for their Sunday round, always the heaviest of all, while their customers lie snug in bed awaiting their regular Sunday fare of "pieces of bodies" or the like.

Spinnakers fill as yachts in the 650-mile Sydney to Hobart ocean race sail through the Heads before a light nor'easter. This is an annual event, held each Boxing Day, and the "start of the Hobart" brings holiday crowds to every harbour vantage point. As a yachting nation Australia is second only to the United States.

Stilt roots of a mangrove are ready-made shelter for these Aborigines of Mornington Island. They have been gathering oysters on the ebbing tide.

This is a profile of Sydney's changing face: older-style, one-family homes, typically red-roofed, give way to high rise units, then to the skyscrapers of the city; to west are the big industrial areas; beyond the one-family suburban homes reappear and spread across the flat plains. Vaucluse, in the foreground, once proudly called a "village", now changing fast as land values continue to soar; Rose Bay, with its small craft and famous flying boats, now under threat; historic Point Piper, and the smoggy city of Sydney.

self-sufficient...

In the cities and larger towns you will find the typical Australian paper boys. They are young, noisy, cheerful and efficient; they don't expect to be tipped but are sometimes slow with the change when serving cars in moving traffic and usually make a point of calling on their early morning customers, around Christmas time, to extend the season's greetings. Australian laws prohibit the employment of youngsters below school leaving age, but a blind eye is turned on the boy selling papers before and after school. It is regarded as typical Australian initiative, and a "paper run" is eagerly sought, by no means the prerogative of the lad "helping a widowed mother". In this commercial age, he is most likely helping himself, with a transistor or surf board in his eye and his money carefully banked towards that end. In the evenings he operates from a fixed vantage point on the homeward path of the city's workers, and the afternoon air rings with his very loud and usually unintelligible cry: "wirrawirra, sunnamirra . . ." as it was once recorded (*Sun* and *Mirror*, Sydney's two evening papers). On winter mornings he is up before daylight, rugged against the frost, pedalling furiously round his "run", lobbing the rolled newspapers accurately on the lawn with a thought to the repercussions of ruined rhododendrons in Melbourne's suburbia. And sometimes, sadly, he is being replaced in this mechanised age by the revving of doorless cars and the stacatto thuds of papers wildly flaying foliage left and right.

The blue singlet or "Jackie Howe" is almost a uniform with Australian outdoor workers. The colloquial name refers to champion blade shearer, Jack Howe, who "shore 327 ewes in 7 hours 20 minutes at Alice Downs (Qld), in October, 1892." He was recognised as the world's greatest hand-shearer, and, it is said, always wore a sleeveless singlet or a shirt with the sleeves cut off. Today it is high fashion with teenage girls, who wear it more proudly than Jackie Howe ever could. Tasmanian roadworker, tough, weatherbeaten, grey-haired, wearing the traditional "Jackie Howe".

Australian women have played a magnificent part in a tough country; their courage and the hardships they have endured is graven on their faces. Such a person is Mrs McDaniels of Broome, Western Australia, whose life has been one of happiness, tragedy and triumph.

Australia's complete individualist: the swagman who turns his back on the crowded city and carries his meagre possessions along the never-ending track. The traditional swagman is becoming rare today, but these charming and gentle fellows of the road are still seen at times. This photograph was taken at dusk at Bateman's Bay; kookaburras were laughing as the interesting and philosophical personality tramped past the spotted gums.

Aboriginal man and his wives near the Musgrave Ranges, South Australia.

Sacred Aboriginal cave paintings at Sleisbeck, Arnhem Land. This is Nargorkun, creator of all the earth and its people, pictured with his two wives.

Some Aboriginal art is purely secular, recording events of the day, and caves are the archives of the community.

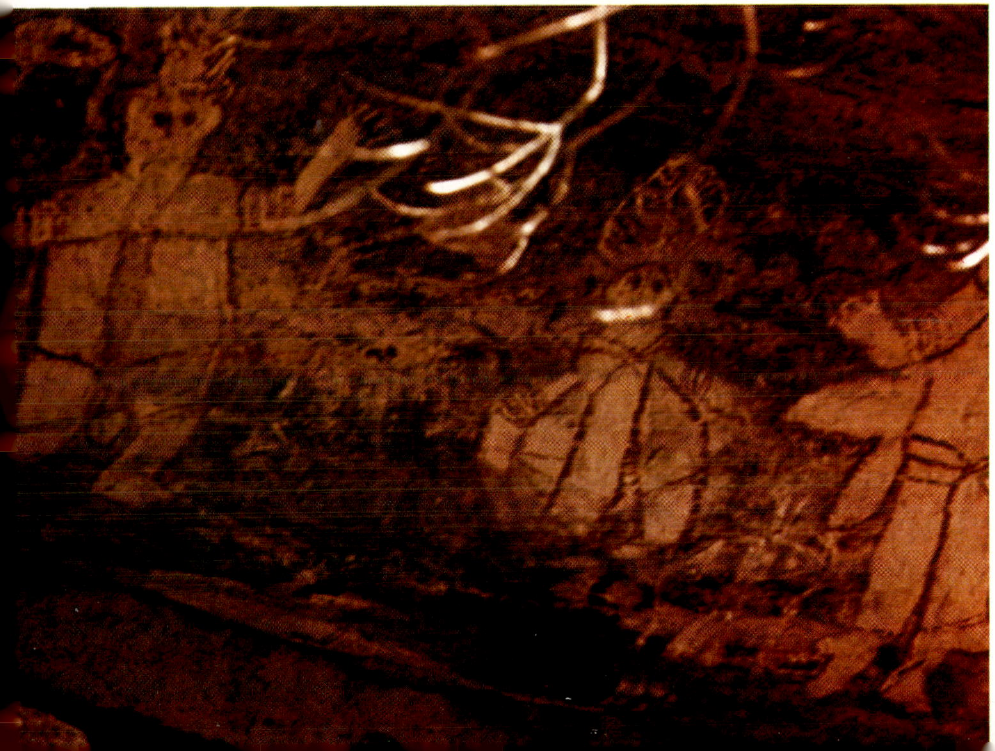

Undisturbed by outside influence for countless centuries, the Aborigine developed a pattern of living and social behaviour which proved remarkably stable and ensured survival with minimum interference with the environment. Marjorie Barnard, who wrote the historical foreword to this book, says of the black Australian and his relationship to his land: "Their adjustment was so complete, so intricate, so completely passed over into their legend and their unconscious mind that they, after thousands of years, had ceased to be interlopers, masters or slaves, and had become a part of the very soil's rhythm, their life a bush pattern, a pattern that after immemorial time we broke past mending in a few years . . ."
Indeed, the Bush looms large in the life of all Australians. Though most are clustered round the coast, they live always in the shadow of the vast wide land behind them. Marjorie Barnard continues: "There is an indelible print on the Australian consciousness of space and distance. Even if he lives in a cramped slum, the Australian knows on some deep level of his mind that his is a big world. When he goes to Europe he runs at once into the size and emptiness of his continent. Fundamentally it is this awareness of the continental mass that makes of the Australian abroad an exile. It becomes in the transplanted a peculiar form of home sickness."
James McAuley expresses it in a different way:

"Yet, as a wheel that's driven in the ruts
It has a wet rim where the people clot
Like mud; and though they
praise the inner spaces,
When asked to go themselves, they'd rather not."

It's a big wheel, anyhow—twelve thousand miles of it. Even if three-quarters of the population live within thirty-five miles of the rim (1971 census) the mud spins thin in places, and thirty-five miles is not far these days.
The bush picnic has always been very much part of Australian urban life. Mum, dad and the kids pack into the car and join the crawl along the crowded roads that snake their way out of the cities and into the bush, there to grill steak and sausages over an open fire and drink the traditional, smoky, "billy" tea, fight the bull-ants and blowflies, and dread the prospect of the bumper-to-bumper crawl back home. In spite of the drawbacks, they return renewed and refreshed by their contact with the land and the open spaces with which they identify, almost as strongly, in their own way, as do the first Australians, the Aborigines.

City and country meet at the Royal Easter Show, when the vast and varied produce of the land is on display; the view at child's eye level, however, is balloons, fairy floss and sample bags.

Aboriginal women at Elcho Island, Northern Territory, play "string games", weaving intricate patterns, each representing everyday actions and objects.

Australian rules, as played by young Aborigines at Elcho Island. This spectacular code of football originated in Melbourne in the eighteen-fifties and has a greater following, per head of population, than any other field sport in the world.

The smiling, freckled face of a typical young Australian country boy.

Aboriginal children play in a dugout canoe, Bathurst Island, Northern Territory.

Aboriginal "sing-sing", a communal "play-about" corroboree, at Arnhem Bay, Northern Territory. These are attended by all, and the women dance with the babies on their shoulders, swaying half-asleep in the flickering firelight to the drone of the didgeridoo and the beat of the clap-stick boomerangs.

mates and mixers...

Of the Australian character, Marjorie Barnard writes:
"The scientist will tell you, as likely as not, that people do not change appreciably in the solar moment of less than two centuries. They do not change radically, but their environment selects and spotlights traits already present . . . Australian circumstance selects certain traits from the Ango-Saxon stock, for emphasis, others the Australian sun is bleaching out . . .
"In the bush, distance and rainfall and time-distance between rains, condition life, and those conditions, so wide, so implacable, make men. The difficult fertility of the earth spaces out habitations, and because men are scattered, neighbourliness ceases to be a virtue and becomes a necessity . . . The rainfall that can turn a desert into a field of daisies and back again makes existence itself a gamble and breeds a race of philosophers and gamblers."
Even in the earliest days, Australians started to regard themselves as something different from the "new chum" and the "pommy". The bewailing convict in "Moreton Bay" proclaims himself a native of Erin's Island but in the "Lime Juice Tub" the "native" Australian exhorts the "pom" to return whence he came. In the face of common hardship and shared struggle, national distinctions eroded quickly to an Australian consciousness; to the predominantly British, predominantly rebellious stock, the environment grafted the Australian ethos of "fair go" and "give it a go"—a mixture of mateship, recklessness and initiative.

A country clearing sale in Australia is a unique and exciting event. Everyone comes, from hundreds of miles around, and everything's sold, from the cattle dog to the station manager's double bed; from stud bulls and heavy machinery to a chipped enamel mug and Great Aunt Maude's painting of pansies. It is a carnival atmosphere tinged with sadness, where friends and neighbours meet amid the debris of generations, spread out between the mindless sun and soil, on sale to the highest bidder. Clearing sale at Slapdash Station, Mudgee district, New South Wales.

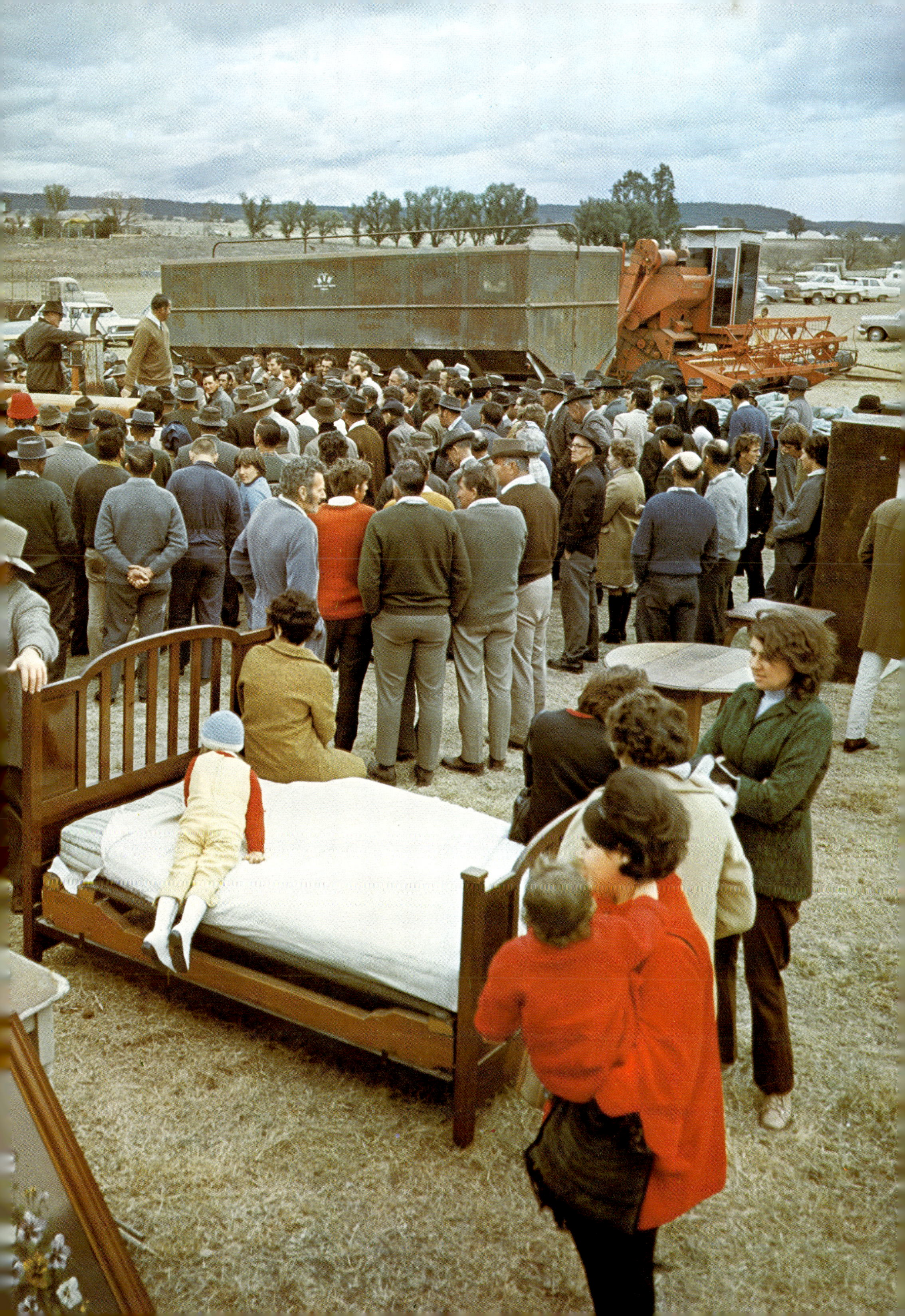

The lined face and defiant eyes of this man reflect the tenacity, courage and obstinate refusal to give way in the face of adversity so characteristic of the "out-back" Australian.

City barrow man, in the "dinkum clobber" of his trade—leather apron and braces—displays his wares on simple but functional tables made from fruit boxes. Balmain, New South Wales.

Australia is a dry land, and hot; the canvas waterbag is essential equipment for those heading inland. Evaporation on the damp surface keeps the water cool on the hottest days. Camooweal, Queensland.

rebels and loners...

Pure recklessness was perhaps the most important element. In the pioneering days men faced enormous odds, either because they had no idea of the odds they were facing or because they had so little to lose they didn't care. Escaped convicts made incredible journeys, seeking China "just over the horizon"; became the "wild white men" of north Queensland and southern Victoria. Bushrangers sang of "together we will plunder, together we will die" and mostly did. In hindsight the "ill-fated" explorers who perished in the interior were as ill-fated as a man making a parachute jump without a parachute. Would Australians have attempted half the struggles they did if they knew what they faced?

"Oh, then their hearts were bolder,
And if Dame Fortune frowned
Their swags they'd lightly shoulder
And tramp to other ground.
Oh, they were lion-hearted
Who gave our country birth!
Stout sons, of stoutest fathers born,
From all the lands of earth."

Or perhaps it was just the great Australian instinct for gambling. Australia is a nation "on the punt", a nation of lottery ticket buyers (where else have they built an Opera House this way?). Our first hospital was built on rum and most hospitals today are subsidised by State-sponsored gambling. Spectacular temples

Tropical cyclones hundreds of miles out to sea send the surf thundering down on Australia's east coach beaches. Palm Beach, New South Wales.

Horse-riding amid snowdrifts and alpine flowers in the tops area, Australian Alps, in summertime.

A sudden southerly buster belts across the harbour and bowls over the eighteen-footer sailing skiffs. One after the other the helmsman is defeated as the boisterous wind overturns his yacht. Three have come to grief here on Sydney Harbour, New South Wales.

of food, drink and entertainment — the "Clubs" — are built and financed by serried ranks of glittering poker machines. "You can't win it if you're not in it" is a national slogan. Phar Lap, a racehorse, is a national hero, his heart preserved at the Institute of Anatomy, Canberra, and his magnificently stuffed hide at Melbourne's National Museum where it is still a major attraction forty years after his death. "Melbourne Cup" day is a State holiday and the whole nation stops for half an hour at three o'clock on the afternoon of the second Tuesday in November — probably closer to a true "national day" than any other. "Two-up" or "swy" (or, as the police quaintly phrase it, "heading them" — a term rarely used by players) has been called the Australian national game. It is illegal, but this is facetiously attributed to the inability of Governments to work out a way to collect money on the bets. Derived from the old convict game of "pitch and toss", all that's needed to play it is a flat piece of ground, a flat piece of wood about the size and shape of a butter pat (the "kip"), two pennies and a gathering of gamblers. The "spinner" tosses the pennies with the kip, the heads (of the watchers) go up, and if heads come down, the spinner collects. If odds, he keeps spinning, if tails he pays out and passes on the kip.

Horse-riding in autumn, near Cotter Dam, Canberra, A.C.T.

"I am going to knock them," screams the stock auctioneer at the country sheep and cattle sales. "Come on you butchers, what about this lot!" Australian auctioneers are colourful individualists, highly entertaining in action — and deadly efficient at getting their price.

A183

Left: *Night corroboree, Arnhem Land, Northern Territory. The Aboriginal people of Australia are determined to preserve their traditional culture.*

Lifesavers parade at surf carnival, Collaroy beach, New South Wales. As indicated by the flags carried, clubs from all States are represented. The pomp and ceremony of the "march past" continues despite the drama of an overturned boat in the pounding surf beyond.

Above: *Dancing round the huge maypole at the Barossa Vintage Festival in the wine-growing Barossa Valley, South Australia. The wine industry was established here in the first half of last century, mosty by settlers from Germany, and colourful German customs survive to the present day among their fifth generation Australian descendants.*

easy-going...

Thousands of miles of beaches scallop the "wet rim". Some near the cities are always crowded, some are almost deserted. The beaches belong to everyone. If you told an Australian that he would henceforth have to pay to go on his own beaches in his own country (as is the case in many places in Europe) he would probably say: "You've got to be joking!"

The beach is pleasure, recreation, exercise, social life and, among young people, almost a cult. The waves roll into the shore . . . smashing waves, high dumpers, long sloping waves. Until the second world war, body surfing was the main sport, and young Australians early learnt the knack of catching the waves and riding them without benefit of a board. Children and the less experienced used small blown-up rubber surf floats to shoot the breakers into shore.

Board surfing was a "late starter" in Australia, comparatively slow to catch on. It originated in Hawaii, where early European visitors were fascinated by the sight of the local inhabitants challenging the wild surf with tree trunks and planks. With the postwar development of lighter, shorter boards, more easily transported, however, it quickly ousted body surfing in popularity, and by 1963, when the first world championships were organised, they were held, not in Hawaii, traditional home of board surfing, but in Australia, and were won by a young Australian, Bernard ("Midge") Farrelly.

Australian beaches are patrolled by volunteer lifesavers. They man the reels and rescue boats when swimmers get into difficulties, and stage the colourful surf carnivals, with "march pasts", rescue and resuscitation drills, boat and surf races, which are so much part of the Australian tradition. But the popularity of board riding and increasing mobility of the young in an age of motor cars is threatening the tradition. Not so many join the lifesaving clubs today, and loyalty to one beach is becoming a thing of the past.

City lunch hour at Martin Plaza, newly formed haven of green trees and bright flowers in the heart of Sydney. Shoppers, students and young city office workers take a lunch break in the sun.

CITY OF SYDNEY

An old bushman in tattered coat turns his back on the cities and heads for the open spaces, pushing his bike.

Paddington, inner suburb of Sydney, has had a chequered career but its interesting Victorian terrace houses are now being restored.

Race meeting at Royal Randwick. Country men, with their broad-brimmed hats and typical stance, stand out among the city crowds like a bull in a china shop.

bush myth...

Australia is a split personality land, and her people also. In this young and ancient land—"They call her a young country, but they lie: She is the last of lands, the emptiest . . ."—the people are both placid and aggressive, conservative and rebellious. They respond to "Waltzing Matilda" rather than "Advance Australia Fair", prefer to identify with the sheep-stealing swaggie on the track to mouthing what they regard as pompous and stilted nationalistic jingle. They made millionaires of successful cattle thieves and affect to despise them; they hung and glorified the unsuccessful:

" 'Come out of that, Ned Kelly,
  you done a lawless thing:
You robbed and fought the squatters.
  Ned Kelly, you must swing.'
'If those who rob', says Kelly,
  'are all condemned to die,
You had better hang the squatters;
  they've stolen more than I.' "

Australian literature shows sympathy for the convicts, the law-breaker, the "underdog", and an almost universal Australian characteristic is distrust of the "cops". Ned Kelly, Australia's foremost folk hero, was a petty horse thief, bank robber and bushranger. The unofficial national anthem applauds the battler in his gallant opposition to the forces of law and private property.

Yet Australians seek respectability though they categorize it with the peculiarly Australian derogatory label of "wowserism". They see themselves as an outdoor people and are proud and very conscious of their bush traditions, yet they live in the most highly urbanised country in the world—much more so than England and America. More than half the total population live in the capital cities; four out of every five Australians are classed as urban. White-collar workers are more than half the workforce, and most of the rest are "blue-collar" industrial workers. Only one in ten works on the land.

White sails of Sydney's Opera House reflect the green of leafy treeferns in the Royal Botanic Gardens in the foreground.

Deserted main street of Tibooburra in the far west of New South Wales. This is the country explored by Sturt and lies near the fringe of the Stony Desert named for him. Tibooburra roars to life when the people from the remote stations come to town, the focal point being the pub.

Canberra, Australia's national capital, is a planned city, designed and built as the seat of Government and set amid outstanding natural and man-made beauty. View from Black Mountain, across man-made Lake Burley Griffin.

The commercial, business and shopping heart of Canberra is Canberra City, centred around City Hill on the northern side of Lake Burley Griffin. Monaro Mall and Friday night shopping, Canberra City.

suburban reality...

Donald Horne describes Australia as "the first suburban nation" and indeed the cities and towns are more collections of suburbs than urban centres; they spread over a greater area for their population than any other cities in the world. Few Australians would agree that theirs is a conformist society, but this is the truth. The common ideal is to "own your own home"—though in practice few ever do, for with this in mind most incur debts they can never pay off in one lifetime, and three-quarters of the houses in Australia are "owner-occupied". They insist that their home be surrounded by its own individual block of land, increase their "nine-to-five" working week by hours of travelling to achieve this, then spend the weekends pushing a lawnmower. They even transfer this ideal to their own little bit of "bush", and the lawnmower is lugged up along with the fishing gear to the "weekender" somewhere along the coastline, an hour or so's drive from the city.

Yet the paradox people of this paradox land still stubbornly cling to their links with the land their fathers or grandfathers left. The "drift to the cities" ebbs and flows with the "drift to the bush" as the footloose young decide to see their land before they settle down; their elders hook caravans to cars and set off to see it after they retire; economic success turns city businessmen to "Pitt Street farmers" and economic recession sends city workers on the track. They all share the same dream. Bush balladist Banjo Paterson, who spent his boyhood in the country and most of his adult life at an office desk in the city, expressed it:

"In my wild erratic fancy
  visions come to me of Clancy
Gone a-droving 'down the Cooper'
  where the Western drovers go;
As the stock are slowly stringing,
  Clancy rides behind them singing,
For the drover's life has pleasures
  that the townsfolk never know.
". . . And I somehow rather fancy
  that I'd like to change with Clancy,
Like to take a turn at droving
  where the seasons come and go,
While *he* faced the round eternal
  of the cash-book and the journal—
But I doubt he'd suit the office,
  Clancy, of The Overflow."

tuated almost in the geographic centre the continent is Alice Springs, the large d rapidly growing urban and tourist ntre of the inland. The occasional mel train is still to be seen in the city reets, reminder of the part these imals and their Afghan drivers played in e development of Australia's interior.

elow: Brisbane, capital of Queensland, is open-hearted city. The people are endly and outgoing, the architecture nique and unlike that of any other ustralian capital.

"Waltzing matilda" means carrying a swag while tramping around looking for work. It is a term made famous by the song of the same name. Banjo Paterson wrote the words after hearing the phrase used in the Winton area of central Queensland (the country depicted on the jacket of the book). Intrigued, he sat down the same night and incorporated it into verses about a "jolly swagman" who camped beside a billabong, grabbed one of the squatter's sheep for tucker when it came down to drink ("And he sang as he shoved that jumbuck in his tucker-bag: 'You'll come a-waltzing Matilda with me!' "), then jumped into the billabong when accosted by the squatter and the "troopers—one—two—three": "And his ghost may be heard as you pass by that billabong: 'You'll come a-waltzing Matilda with me!' " His verses were later set to music to become what many would regard as Australia's theme song.

The Australian "swaggie" as such seems to have originated in the days of the goldrushes. Drifting away from the spent fields of Victoria, New South Wales and Queensland, the diggers joined the ranks of itinerant workers: shearers, fruit-pickers, timbermen and drovers. From these ranks came the swagman, a taciturn man who mostly travelled alone or with a dog. As distinct from that other Australian bush wanderer, the "sundowner" who was alleged to plan his day's tramp so as to arrive at a homestead at dusk thus avoiding the risk of finding work while at the same time ensuring free rations and shelter for the night, the swagman's reputation was one of independence, a man genuinely seeking work, however briefly.

The traditional swaggie was one who was methodical if not meticulous in his manner of dress. His swag or "drum" consisted of the minimum in spare clothing rolled up in a blanket, usually blue (hence the other colloquial term, "humping the bluey"). This was carried on one side of his body and balanced on the other by a sugarbag ("tucker-bag") containing flour, sugar, tea and perhaps meat, and by his old black billy. These were supported by a leather belt wrapped around the bluey and passed over his neck, which was protected by a towel or even a spare pair of long red flannels. His moleskin trousers were held up at the knee by a strip of stringybark or greenhide, and his battered felt hat was ringed with corks to keep off the flies.

The "billy" or "billy-can" was a tin can of varying size, with wire handle attached, used

Hobart, on the Derwent River at the foot of Mount Wellington, Tasmania, is the second oldest city in Australia. It was settled in 1803 as a second penal colony and a counter to possible French aims in the area. Hobart is a city with the tang of the sea; the estuary of the Derwent is one of the finest deepsea harbours in the world, and in the days of whaling one of the most important. Though now a modern and beautiful city, it still retains the aura of history and many pockets of early colonial architecture have been preserved.

Perth, capital of Western Australia, is a city rushing to the skies, with new multi-storied buildings rising on all sides, yet still retains "old world" areas such as London Court with its variety of curiosity shops and boutiques, and preserves at its very heart King's Park, an area of a thousand-odd acres, mostly still in its natural state and a sanctuary for the unique wildflowers of the area.

for making "billy" tea. This also seems to have originated in the goldfields and its name is variously attributed to a "bully" beef can, a French "bouilli" soup can, and the Aboriginal word "billa" (water). Whatever the origin, it is commemorated in many a traditional bush ballad, of which "My Old Black Billy" is typical:

"I've humped my bluey in all the States
With my old black billy, the best of mates.
For years I've camped, and toiled and tramped
Over roads that are rough and hilly,
With my plain and sensible,
Indispensable,
Old black billy."

The swagman's trade, if it can be called that, is one that is almost gone. Itinerant work-seekers of later years are more inclined to carry duffle bags or suitcases, accept lifts from trucks or cars, if they haven't their own "old bomb" for transport. Essentially the swaggie belongs to the age of the horse and buggy; he has no affinity with the rush and bustle of the motor age. But if you travel the roads you will still see the "old-timers" to whom the swaggie's tramp has become a way of life, counted in decades not days. And in the souvenir shops of the tourist centres you will find little mannikins a-plenty to remind us of our folklore: small models of swaggies, complete with all the necessary paraphernalia; tucker-bag, bluey, billy, hat with corks, trousers tied up with string. Wind them up and they tinkle "Waltzing Matilda".

Darwin, seaport and administrative centre of the Northern Territory, is the most cosmopolitan city in Australia. Chinese joss houses rub shoulders with modern buildings and carpets from Persia are sold by auction at colourful open air markets.

Adelaide, capital of South Australia, is a city in quest of culture, venue of the biennial Festival of Arts which attracts top Australian and leading overseas artists and performers. Fountains of Victoria Square, in wide King William Street, are illuminated for the occasion.

Adelaide's earlier reputation was as the "City of Churches" and while it indeed has many of outstanding architecture it also has its fair share of pubs, often strategically placed on the opposite corner. Competition however is regulated; the pubs close on Sundays.

Melbourne and Sydney, the two largest cities in Australia, have a longstanding reputation for rivalry. Sydneysiders maintain that Melbourne is staid and conservative, a stodgy city of stockbrokers where everything shuts down on Sundays and the businessmen probably wear bowler hats and carry furled umbrellas. Melburnians regard their Sydney cousins as loud-mouthed go-getters, as like as not to spend their leisure time lounging in the sun outside the pubs as in the quiet domestic pursuits of the family home.

conservative...

Walk down a busy city street in Australia today, preferably in the lunch hour. You will be struck by the preponderance of youth in the workforce — legacy of the postwar population explosion. You may see a few people of pension age in the crowd, usually alone, but not many middle-aged friends shopping in couples as they used to ("having a day in town together") because now they patronise the big surburban complexes and save expensive fares. The young swing along at their lunch-hour shopping, or meet in groups in the newly-formed plazas — impossible to tell from their clothes, manners or speech whether their fathers are financial mining magnates or wharf labourers (the children probably went to the same school anyway). In the nineteen-seventies the boys have whiskers, sideburns and hair as long as they dare. The girls wear long pants or very short skirts (they obstinately resisted the maxi fashion) blouses that don't always meet at the midriff, high platform-soled shoes. Generally they all look bright, healthy and unworried.

The young city dwellers recognise the popular image of an Australian — a lean, out-of-doors, hatchet-faced, laconic character, seated on a horse with the sheep in front and his dog at the ready, or a bronzed lifesaver stepping it out behind the banner on Bondi beach — but this is not today's world, not theirs, anyway.

Today less than ten per cent of the working population produce the food that suffices both for Australia's needs and the export markets. Even the lifesavers' days are numbered; small power craft with two-way radio are more efficient.

A greater emphasis is being placed on education. The young stay students longer, the young workers are induced by the lure of highly paid jobs to study more, at home or at "tech". They work incredibly hard, and expect incredibly much. Marriage is a practical affair; glance at their hands — many of them, boys and girls alike, are already married and have exchanged rings, adopting a continental custom. The marriage age for both sexes is dropping; young people now vote and can marry without parental consent at eighteen.

Melbourne at dusk, from across the Yarra.

New A.M.P. Building, Melbourne, is an outstanding example of the modern architecture of the business centre.

Royal Hotel, Randwick (Sydney) preserves the delicate iron lacework of an earlier period. Saturday morning drinkers spill out over the footpath into the autumn sunlight.

50¢

gregarious...

Both sexes accept and expect their role as income providers. Together they cheerfully undertake enormous debt to get a block of land, a house, furniture. The car has gone out of the luxury class; it is the essential means of transport to get them to and from their work. Australia has the highest rate of home "ownership" in the world; the third highest rate of car "ownership"; the greatest involvement in hire purchase. But the bank holds the deeds, the finance companies own the car and "frig". On the basis of average earnings—statistically higher than that of the majority of wage-earners—Young Australia in its 'teens and 'twenties blithely mortgages its entire working life. Another facet of the Australian myth of egalitarianism—all expect to be chiefs, there are no indians.

Young lovers by the gay flower stalls of Sydney's Martin Plaza, a quiet spot in the heart of a busy city.

City and country mingle in the all-pervasive atmosphere of cow dung at Sydney's Royal Easter Show. Cattle judges in broad-brimmed hats determine the champions from a line of santa gertrudis.

Adventurous architecture of Sydney's rapidly developing "twin city" on the north shore of the harbour. Built on Sydney's highest ridge, the "crow's nest" of earlier, sea-orientated days, this gaily coloured building can be seen from vantage points many miles away.

The splendour of Victorian-Gothic architecture as preserved and displayed in the E. S. and A. Bank, Melbourne. Melbourne is regarded as the financial centre of Australia, and is famous for her substantial bank buildings.

Both Sydney and Melbourne have colourful "village" type centres and offer a variety of interesting wares in charming individualistic shops such as this one at Sydney's Double Bay.

The congested streets of the inner city contrast oddly with the wide, tree-lined avenues, envy of interstate visitors, which lead into Melbourne. Melbourne clung stubbornly to her trams when other cities discarded them and is now reaping the benefit of pollution-free transport while smog-laden cities elsewhere re-think their decision.

BRASHS
Turner
SAFE-T MOWERS
FRIENDLY
SAFETY ZONE
50
CARS STOP HERE
R.G.WILSON & Co
LICENSED GROCERS
DELIVERY SERVICE
63-8262

Tapping the furnace at Mount Isa, Australia's biggest producer of copper and one of the greatest silver-lead-zinc centres in the world. All four ores comes from one great mine which is the centre of a booming city on the dry spinifex plains of northwest Queensland.

Timber cutters in the Blue Mountains, near Sydney, New South Wales, load logs up to two or three hundred feet long onto timber jinkers. Australia has the tallest hardwood forests in the world.

Gathering bales of hay in the Hunter Valley, New South Wales, one of the richest and most highly developed dairy-farming areas in Australia.

Mechanical corn harvester, Muswellbrook, New South Wales, gathers two, three or four rows at a time, pulling the stalks through rollers and snapping off the cob.

the workers...

Australians are resourceful and inventive. Writes Marjorie Barnard: "The hard ways of the bush, where to be lost is to perish, make the bushman as the sea makes the mariner. When it is learn or die, men learn (or die). In the Australian bush man was thrown back again in the nineteenth century on his own resources. He had to improvise, to create his world from scant materials. He went back centuries, became creative again . . ." Where else but in Australia would anyone think to invent the stump-jump plough? In any other agricultural nation in the world, the intensity of agriculture would have necessitated that the stump be removed. In Australia, where land cost less than the labour to clear it, especially in the "mallee" country where the greatest bulk of the trees are underground, the Australian farmer pitted his wits against the ingenuity of the eucalypt and came up with a plough that jumped the stumps, enabling the land to be used, while the massive roots were progressively removed, without risk of damage to the plough. The stump-jump plough originated in the mallee country of South Australia and was a development on an earlier innovation from the same area—"Mullensing"—where a V-shaped log with spikes driven into the undersurface was dragged over ground from which the light top scrub had been cleared, bouncing over the hidden stumps and burying the seed as it loosened the soil. Combined with the stripper, a mechanical wheat harvester which could operate around low stumps (another development of South Australian mallee—an entirely new process which cut off heads only and stripped and gathered the grain in one process) the stump jump plough and "mullenizer" forced the mallee to share the soil with crops. Perhaps an example of an Australian "near enough's good enough . . . she'll be right Jack" philosophy? Frances Wheelhouse ("Digging Stick to Rotary Hoe") says: "Some claimed that it was slovenly to leave the stumps in the ground. They lost sight of its tremendous economic value while the clearing was in progress." In any case, agricultural inventions, mothered by necessity, are a feature of Australian rural life. The wide variety of machinery available to the Australian farmer in the mid twentieth century prompted Lennie Lower, insouciant Australian humourist, to parody the old bush ballad:

"Wrap me up in my stockwhip and blanket,
And bury me deep down below,
Where the farm implement salesman won't
molest me,
In the place where the cooler bars grow."

Loading wharf at Groote Eylandt, Northern Territory, major centre of manganese production. These wharves run far out to sea, enabling vessels to be loaded at all times despite the high tide fluctuations.

Australia, for the first one hundred and fifty or so years of white settlement, was in the main a rural country. Once the barrier of the Blue Mountains was breached and the colony was no longer confined to the coast, a great expansion of settlement followed. "Squatters", who did their own exploring (sometimes long before the official parties who were often puzzled that the natives they encountered in supposedly unexplored lands showed no surprise at white men and their animals) set up "runs" in defiance of Government attempts to confine them to a manageable "Nineteen Counties". They spread north, south and west from the established settlements, meeting each other in the hinterlands. Then, with closer settlement, came the epic overland treks as the bush pioneers moved great mobs of cattle to stock huge holdings further out—in the north, and the northwest. The bulk of the nation's wealth came from pastoral and agricultural production.

Over the last few decades, however, the emphasis is changing. Manufacturing is expanding, and mining is matching rural production in primary industry. Today Australia is the world's largest exporter of bauxite, and the world's biggest bauxite mine is at Weipa, on Cape York Peninsula—near where the Dutch navigators made their first Australian landfall in 1606. Mountains of high-grade iron ore have an immensely greater value than all the gold mined in Australia since the first rush in the eighteen-fifties. Oil, only a few years ago considered non-existent in payable quantities in Australia, has now been found in Bass Strait, Queensland and the off-shore islands of the West, and is the subject of lively exploration and discovery both on land and on Australia's wide continental shelf. Natural gas has been tapped and is being piped across the continent.

Desert nights are cold and the spinifex grass fire creates a catherine wheel of sparks as the oil exploration team keep warm around the campfire at Wilsons Cliffs, Western Australia. The hundred foot high oil rig is outlined against the flat horizon.

the wealth...

In terms of area, production and export earnings, wheat is the most important crop in Australia. The bulk of the harvest is exported—earning over five hundred million dollars a year—and marketing and storage play an important part in the industry. Sometimes we produce so much there is trouble over surpluses; quotas are set, storage is strained and drought is hailed as a godsend when it cuts production down to manageable levels. Then, the next year, world demand drains the giant silos; drought reverts to its black role and combines with quotas to frustrate the farmers while marketing boards frantically search for the wheat they've oversold. Australia is one of the world's major exporters of grain, and owes this position mainly to the pioneering work done in the breeding of wheat suitable for local conditions. William James Farrer is foremost in this field. Interested in developing a rust and drought-resistant strain, he systematically cross-bred types along lines parallel to Mendel's theory (though independently as he was unaware of the latter's research until much later) and his "Federation" wheat, produced at the turn of the century, was a major advance. His work, and the continued efforts of those who followed him, have proved of immense benefit to the industry.

For most of its history, wool has been the mainstay of Australia's economy. Australia has the largest sheep population of any country in the world (180 million in the peak year, 1970) and is the greatest wool producer,

Giant wheat silo at Parkes, New South Wales, is a quarter of a mile long; the soaring hardwood columns that support it are single lengths cut from huge eucalypts. It empties rapidly in the face of growing demand for Australia's golden grain.

Pearl diver surfaces after an exhausting period on the ocean floor, off the north west coast of Australia. Pearling is a major industry at Broome, Western Australia.

Cotton harvest at Wee Waa, western New South Wales, main cotton-growing centre in Australia.

Smoke from the cane fires spreads over the green countryside at Cairns, Queensland. This is the major sugar-growing area in Australia and in the season, when the cane is fired before cutting, the air is heavy with smoke and the night sky brilliantly illuminated by the glow of the fires.

Shearing the golden fleece at Cassilis, New South Wales.

Huge wool-handling complex at Yennora, New South Wales, covers an area of twenty six acres.

supplying about one third of the total world requirements. Most of this wool is exported, making the industry particularly vulnerable to fluctuations in world demand. In the early nineteen seventies disastrous drops in prices reduced Australia's income from wool to about half what it had been a couple of years previously — though production had remained at the same high level — and half that earned twenty years before, when production was considerably lower! The sheep population was slashed by twenty million, slaughtered for meat as graziers turned their holdings over to beef production. Within twelve months world demand had pushed the price of wool to record levels and in the race to rebuild the decimated flocks lamb became a luxury item and all but disappeared from the Australian dinner table. Wool production is still the major pastoral industry in Australia but is now being nudged rather strongly by beef cattle. Minerals, which are now overtaking rural production as the main source of Australia's wealth, have always played an important part in filling the nation's coffers. Australia's first export was coal, and the industry is still a major income-earner. In the days of the gold rushes Australia produced forty per cent of the world's supplies of the precious mineral. Australia is the world's chief producer of lead and a major producer of zinc, silver and copper. She is self-sufficient in most minerals of economic importance and much more than self-sufficient in some. Bauxite deposits, basis of aluminium, are believed to be the largest in the world; oil and natural gas have been found in a number of sedimentary basins; gigantic deposits of nickel have been discovered. However, it is worth recalling that Australia, at one time the world's largest producer of tin, was later scratching for sufficient to meet domestic requirements. Unlike rural production, mineral resources cannot be renewed. New discoveries may be made, but once slaughtered, you can't breed up the flock.

Offshore drilling rigs probe for oil and natural gas at several points around the Australian coast. Exploration rig, Bass Strait, off the coast of Victoria.

Historic Magill winery in the Adelaide Hills, South Australia, established more than a century ago by pioneer vigneron Dr Penfold.

The red-rusted "waltzing matilda" country of Winton, western Queensland turned green by the single-handed tenacity of one man and his family. This is one of the most spectacular irrigated properties in Australia; it is situated in a semi-arid region where the annual rainfall comes in one great gulp and is lost as quickly to sun and sand. This man stores the rain that falls on his property in two huge irrigation lakes with a combined capacity of over a thousand million gallons.

Forest drowned by desert sands near Lancelin, Western Australia. Unskilled farming can turn marginal lands to deserts, and wholesale slaughter of trees, either for woodchip industry or agricultural exploitation, can turn the whole of Australia into a wasteland.

These hills near Mount Lyell, on Tasmania's west coast, were covered with tall trees and dense vegetation until sulphurous fumes from the copper smelting works there utterly destroyed them. Ironically, this strange man-made devastation has been turned into a tourist attraction.

The Heritage

Australia is the last continent to be settled by man, the last to be ploughed, the last to be "developed". For almost two centuries we lived with a myth of infinite natural resources, racing across the continent as gold rush followed land rush, to be followed in turn by widespread mineral exploration. But the bonanza is almost over; the harvest of Australia's resources, both renewable and finite, is now a matter for urgent scientific research and careful husbandry. Already we have paid a heavy price in the name of progress. The ravages of land misuse— over-clearing, over-stocking, over-grazing— have turned delicately balanced ecologies to near desert; exploitation of mineral resources threaten to crush the very landscape itself and cart it to dumps halfway across the world. And the quite remarkable surge of public concern in recent years demonstrates that Australians are no longer prepared to "stump-jump" the problems of conservation. The land "over the next hill" is running out; the only frontiers now lie within the human mind. The problems are formidable, but the challenge is being met. Driest of continents, Australia is by no means completely arid. Its vast area collects immense volumes of surface water, most of which is lost by evaporation or poured wastefully into the sea. Rainfall is seasonal and erratic in many areas but it does fall; much of our so-called desert regions receive on the average sufficient rain to support, with careful planning and husbandry, moderate grazing and agricultural activities. Australia's semi-arid areas also possess that greatest asset of all—abundant sunshine. Though it parches the soil and the soul of the farmer, sunshine, along with water and air, is the basic element of life. Australia is also fortunate in that great artesian basins of subterranean water underlie most of the arid areas in the interior.

Pictured on these pages are examples of man's endeavours to develop and conserve the natural renewable resources of the land, enlisting nature's aid instead of engaging in constant conflict with her—and of the results of man's efforts to "conquer" the land, to extract the maximum return in the minimum time without regard for the past or the future. The property pictured on the opposite page is in a low rainfall area; the landholder determined to hold every drop that fell, utilising land shapes to store it and then channel it as needed during the long dry months that lie between the seasonal deluges. This type of water conservation is within the reach of every landowner—and reduces the need for multi-million dollar dams and expensive reticulation over hundreds of miles. Its keynote is holding the water where it falls.

Wheat farms, Eyre Peninsula, South Australia. Here belts of trees have been left in an attempt to protect the wheatfields from wind erosion and provide a habitat for the birds that can control insect pests.

The beautiful Talbingo Valley in the Great Dividing Range, New South Wales.

Idyllic Australian country scene: a pigtailed girl rounds up a rogue steer.

Undulating country at the foot of the Great Divide, Ararat, Victoria; haystooks lie on the fields in this rich grain and wine-producing country.

William Hatfield, in *Australia Reclaimed,* wrote: "Australia has *not* 'ridden on the sheep's back . . .' The sheep has simply trampled across its face!" Australia's mammoth sheep population — a dozen or more for every man, woman and child in the country — has indeed been the mainstay of Australia's economy for most of its economic history, but at a cost not yet fully computed. Most of Australia's sheep are run on marginal land — this was the great "break-through" that sent the industry booming, the development of the hardy Australian strain of fine wool producers that could flourish even in salt-bush country with less than ten inches rainfall. Over-optimistic stocking based on "good" years meant that in the inevitable "bad" years a hundred million or more mouths searched out roots as well as herbage, while four times that number of hooves trampled the bare soil to dust. Wheat, Australia's major agricultural crop, also has a case to answer: following the development of drought-resistant Australian strains, vast areas were cleared and sown to wheat alone. One-crop farming places intolerable burdens on the soil, eventually dooming the land to desert.

Has Australia "ridden on the sheep's back"—or has the sheep simply trampled across its face? The hardy eucalypts are still topped with greenery, but starving sheep have left no trace of vegetation at ground level. Overstocking ruins both the land and the grazier.

This animal has been slaughtered for its skin, and the carcase left to rot on the ground — the mark of the amateur, rather than the professional shooter.

A kindlier aspect of man and the kangaroo; driver of one of the giant road trains that travel the beef roads of Australia's north shares his lunch with a small fellow-traveller.

Professional 'roo hunter from Coonamble, with gutted carcases for the pets' food industry. To the professional this is a trade; he kills selectively and does not leave carcases to pollute the countryside.

Australia's wildlife is under threat — slaughtered for pelts or pet's meat, harassed by introduced predators, doomed by destruction of its habitat. Almost half of the macropod species which existed in eastern Australia when Captain Cook sailed up the coast less than two centuries ago are now either extinct or so rare as to be on the verge of extinction. Only a half-dozen species are classed as common, and these are the larger animals which survived the fox and feral cat but are now coming into increasing conflict with man.

The kangaroo populations of inland areas are a matter of some controversy. These are the largest marsupials and range widely over the continent. There are four main species — the eastern grey or forester, an inhabitant of the coastal forests and tablelands of eastern Australia; the western grey, which ranges from Western Australia to South Australia; the wallaroo or euro, found in hilly forested areas throughout the continent, and the big red, which roams the inland plains.

These animals are herbivores, relatively large and mobile. Development of land for grazing and cropping soon brings them into confrontation with man. Fences are damaged, maturing crops flattened as they move in numbers along the same tracks; the grazier fears they are robbing his stock of the improved pastures he has provided as well as competing with them for the natural herbage. Of the four, probably the euro is safest, mainly because he inhabits areas less favoured by both farmers and commercial hunters, and the grey in the greatest danger, for he seeks to live in the land man finds most attractive. All are still classed as common—indeed in some areas man's interference with the environment has widened the animals' scope, such as by the provision of dams and watering places where none existed before — but unless the basic conflict between kangaroo and farmer can be solved, they are in danger. Part of the answer is in the provision of permanent reserves and parks to preserve as far as possible the natural habitats of Australia's wildlife, and this has been done increasingly throughout the Commonwealth, reflecting the growing awareness of all Australians in the future of their wildlife. Another answer could be in the controlled cropping under licence and their complete protection apart from this. Rather than be left rotting on the ground as agricultural pests, animals culled could be used for man's benefit — the animal that is useful to man has the greatest chance of survival.

Tasmanian wallaby with a joey almost as big as herself. When faced with the "threat" of the camera, the youngster hopefully tries to regain the security of its mother's pouch.

Scarlet-flowered gum; eucalypts predominate in the Australian bush and there are over three hundred different species, ranging from dwarf shrubs to giant trees.

The Leichhardt tree, photographed blooming beside the Mitchell River, Cape York Peninsula, Queensland. This strange and beautiful flower is found only in Queensland's tropical rainforests, and is known to have medicinal properties.

The bush rose is a small mallee-type eucalypt of Western Australia. It grows as a small stunted bush but its flower is one of the largest and most spectacular of all the eucalypts: crimson, gold-tipped and three or more inches across.

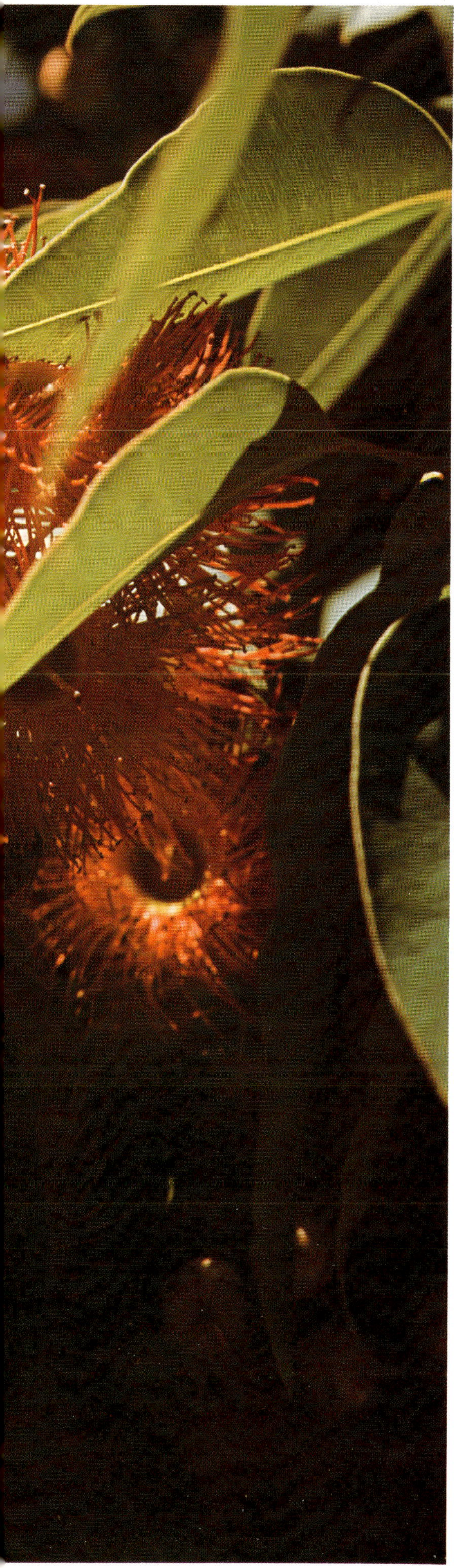

acknowledgements...

At night the Australian bush is alive with the activities of tiny nocturnal marsupials such as the sugar glider. Membranes between the fore and hind limbs enable these little animals to glide remarkable distances from tree to tree in search of their diet of insects, nectar and native fruits.

The Glasshouse Mountains, just north of Brisbane, Queensland, are remnant spines of ancient volcanoes. Only the harder lava of the plugs remain, to form a spectacular series of bare rocky peaks. They were named by Captain Cook, who sighted the strange formations when he sailed up the coast in 1770.

For permission to reproduce Dorothea Mackellar's "My Country" thanks are due to the estate of the late Dorothea Mackellar and Curtis Brown (Aust) Pty Ltd. The verses quoted on page 50 are from "Australian Scenery" by A. B. Paterson; on page 53 from "Distant Land" by Dudley Rannard; on page 95 from "The Broken-Down Squatter," an old bush ballad; on page 101 from James McAuley's "Under Aldebaran"; on page 101 from "The Roaring Days" by Henry Lawson; on page 111 from "Last of Lands" by A. D. Hope and "The Death of Ned Kelly" by John Manifold; on page 115 from "Clancy of the Overflow" by A. B. Paterson; on page 129 from "Here's Luck" by Lennie Lower (a parody of the old bush ballad, "The Dying Stockman," the last two lines of which are:
"Where the dingoes and crows can't molest me,
In the shade where the coolibahs grow.")
Extracts quoted on pages 95, 98 and 129 are from "Australian Outline" by Marjorie Barnard. The farming method employed at Winton (page 267) is P. A. Yeoman's keyline system.
The authors wish to extend their sincere thanks to the following—Nandjawarra, O.B.E., of Groote Eylandt, and many other Aboriginal friends; Colonel Michael Casy of Groote Eylandt, Rev. Shepherdson of Elcho Island, Rev. Doug Belcher of Mornington Island, Rev. Sherlock; Mr Giese and Mr Milliken of the Welfare Department, Darwin; Professor John Cawte, Elizabeth Pope, the Director and staff of the Australian Museum, Dr Mary Tindale, the Director and staff of the National Herbarium of New South Wales, Dr D. L. Serventy, Vincent Serventy, Eric Worrell; the late Sir Edward Hallstrom, Peter Baillieu, Dick Dumbrell, John Davis, Geoff Goddard, Alan Grant, Ron Milne, Keith Tweedy, Sandra and Oke Blomquist, John Barrie, Tom Watson, Jeremy Long, Fred Sutton, Vic Parkinson; Eddie Connellan of Connellan Airways, Jack Hunt and Don Adams of Island Airways, Helmit Apitz, Dr John Morris, Jack Parker and the many other intrepid seamen and pilots who made the book possible; Ron Israel, Maureen McGrath, Betty Maloney, Andrew and Margaret Martin, Elfrida Morcomb, Enid Dumbrell, Elaine Baglin and Bill Mullins. Photographs of Heard Island were taken by the South Indian Ocean Expedition to Heard Island, 1964-65.

DON'T RUBBISH
AUSTRALIA!